NOTICE:
Warning of Copyright Restrictions

Get started
in Dutch

Gerdi Quist and Dennis Strik

Teach®
Yourself

Get started
in Dutch

Gerdi Quist and Dennis Strik

**Also available
in ebook**

Contents

Meet the authors

Gerdi and Dennis are highly experienced language teachers and authors. Gerdi is lecturer in Dutch at University College London, and conducts research into language teaching in general, and Dutch in particular, focusing on intercultural communication. Dennis worked as a lecturer in Dutch at UCL for ten years, before moving back to the Netherlands, where he continues to write language books, teaches Dutch and works as a professional translator.

Together Gerdi and Dennis have written a whole range of language course books for learners at all levels, from beginners to advanced learners at an academic level, both for self-study purposes and classroom environments. Amongst the titles Gerdi and Dennis have produced are *Get started in Dutch* and *Complete Dutch*, published by Hodder Education, aimed at beginners and students at intermediate level, and the *Routledge Intensive Dutch Course*, which is intended for academic learners.

How this book works

Before you start

Read this introduction. It will give you some general information and an idea of how the book is structured and how to approach the course. It also gives you a few tips for learning.

WHAT'S IN A NAME?

Dutch is the name of the official language spoken in the Netherlands and in the Dutch-speaking northern part of Belgium, Flanders. This whole area is sometimes referred to as the Low Countries. Over 20 million people speak Dutch as their first language, so it is by no means a minority language.

The Netherlands is also frequently referred to as Holland, particularly in sporting competitions. However, strictly speaking, the name Holland refers only to the two western provinces (Noord-Holland and Zuid-Holland). Dutch people living outside this area might well correct you if you refer to their country as Holland. Dutch is learnt and studied worldwide by many people and, contrary to what many Dutch would have you believe, it is a relatively easy language to learn, particularly for speakers of English, owing to the many similarities in vocabulary and the regularities of the language.

WHAT'S THIS BOOK ABOUT?

This book is designed for beginners of Dutch who have little or no previous language-learning experience. It aims to introduce you to the basics of the Dutch language and to give you some insight into Dutch (and to a lesser extent Flemish) culture. The book aims to help you in communicating in real-life situations and conversations; not just to give you phrases for shopping and ordering food, but to give you the basics for creating your own messages and meanings. To do this, this extensively revised edition introduces you to grammatical patterns, vocabulary and expressions which are used frequently in the Low Countries. To communicate naturally with native speakers it is also very important that you understand what things are (usually) said or cannot be said in certain situations. To this end we have included some information about this, particularly about the level of informality of certain ways of saying things. By the end of the course you should have acquired enough language to engage in simple conversations and to read some basic and straightforward texts.

HOW IS IT STRUCTURED?

This book is structured progressively throughout. It is structured in such a way that initially you learn simple language patterns which you can apply to many different situations. Each unit builds on the previous ones and gradually you will be learning new language patterns and vocabulary across a variety of topics and situations.

There are ten units. At the beginning of each unit there are sections giving you lots of useful information about the Dutch way of life which generally avoid the typical tourist information you will find in any tourist guide, but instead tell you about conventions and trends in such topics as eating, holidays or values in general in the Low Countries. The units contain dialogues, a large number of exercises or activities and various explanations. At the back of the book, you will find a Grammar summary which explains the basic rules of Dutch grammar.

HOW DO YOU LEARN A NEW LANGUAGE?

Unfortunately, there is no foolproof way of learning a new language.

Different people learn in different ways. Some may prefer to learn about the rules of the language and to practise these. Others may prefer to start talking with native speakers as soon as possible and to learn phrases which they can use in real life immediately. This course is designed to cater for both these ways of learning. In general, though, it is a good idea if you use as many different strategies as possible. It may help you to memorize all the different words and patterns you have learnt, or you may want to practise the different patterns with the new vocabulary or new situations you encounter. Clearly, if you learn a new language, it does mean you will need to invest some time in it. The only way for language to stick is to practise and preferably use it in real situations. But in most cases of learning a foreign language you will have to make do with second best: exercises to help you to communicate.

It is important that you practise regularly, because each unit will include some of the new words and patterns which you have learnt in the previous units. It is better to practise only half an hour a day than one three-hour session a week.

Finally, learning a new language from a self-study book is clearly no substitute for attending classes, where you can communicate in Dutch with the teacher and other students. Ideally, you should take every opportunity available to talk in Dutch with a (near) native speaker and to read or listen to authentic Dutch material. It might also help if you can get hold of a children's book with a recording. You will then be able to listen and read at the same time. Not all children's books are interesting for adults, but in recent years some good books have been published, even for the younger age range. The advantage of these is that the language used is simple, but authentic and up to date.

HOW TO LEARN NEW VOCABULARY

Learning many new words can be a daunting task, particularly if you haven't learnt a foreign language before. Many people devise their own strategies to help them in learning new words. This could be recording the new words and listening to them while you are in the car or doing chores around the house. It could be writing words on Post-its and sticking them around the house, bathroom or wherever you will see them regularly. One thing you should do is to make a vocabulary list yourself of all the new words you encounter. Even though there is a vocabulary list at the end of this book, the advantage of having your own list is that you can group the words in a way that makes it easier to remember for you. You could group words around topic areas or you could group words grammatically, e.g. verbs, nouns, etc., whatever makes it logical for you. It is important that whenever you list a word, you list it with an example sentence (or two) so that you can learn the word in the context(s) in which it is used.

SPELLING RULES

Many people find these rules difficult, particularly before they know much Dutch. If you see spellings in the first few units that seem to change and that you can't understand, you can refer to these rules for guidance. However, if at first you still remain confused, stick to the main spelling of the word that you find in the vocabulary list. Later, however, you will have to get to grips with these rules.

SYMBOLS USED IN THIS BOOK

Listen to audio

Speak – speak Dutch out loud (even if you're alone)

Pronunciation icon

Culture tip

Reading passage

Write and make notes

Learn to learn

The Discovery method

There are lots of approaches to language learning, some practical, some quite unconventional. Perhaps you know of a few, or even have some techniques of your own. In this book we have incorporated the **Discovery method** of learning, a sort of DIY approach to language learning. What this means is that you will be encouraged throughout the course to engage your mind and figure out the language for yourself, through identifying patterns, understanding grammar concepts, noticing words that are similar to English and more. This method promotes language awareness, a critical skill in acquiring a new language. As a result of your own efforts, you will be able to better retain what you have learnt, use it with confidence, and, even better, apply those same skills to continuing to learn the language (or, indeed, another one) on your own after you've finished this course.

Everyone can succeed in learning a language – the key is to know how to learn it. Learning is more than just reading or memorizing grammar and vocabulary. It's about being an active learner, learning in real contexts, and, most importantly, using what you've learnt in different situations. Simply put, if you figure something out for yourself, you're more likely to understand it. And when you use what you've learnt, you're more likely to remember it. And because many of the essential but (let's admit it!) dull details, such as grammar rules, are introduced through the Discovery method, you'll have more fun while learning. Soon, the language will start to make sense and you'll be relying on your own intuition to construct original sentences independently, not just listening and repeating.

Enjoy yourself!

The Dutch Language

Dutch is the official language of the Netherlands and one of the official languages of Belgium, where it is spoken in the northern region of Flanders. Many people, particularly the Dutch, tend to claim it is a difficult language to learn, but in fact it is a lot more regular than, say, English, and it isn't as complicated as German.

Spelling

There is only one major spelling rule to learn, which concerns the vowel sounds **a**, **e**, **o** and **u**.

Short vowel sounds are always spelt with one letter and always occur in a closed syllable (a syllable ending in a consonant).

man *man*   **lek** *leak*   **bot** *bone*   **kus** *kiss*

Long vowel sounds can be spelt either with two letters (as in the examples) or one letter (**a**, **e**, **o**, **u**), depending on whether they appear in a closed syllable (ending in a consonant) or an open syllable (ending in a vowel).

maan *moon*   **leek** *layman*   **boot** *boat*   **vuur** *fire*

The long vowel sounds are always spelt with two letters in closed syllables. When they appear in an open syllable, they are spelt with a single letter. This happens, for instance, when **-en** is added to make words plural:

maan *moon*   **leek** *layman*   **boot** *boat*   **vuur** *fire*
manen *moons*   **leken** *laymen*   **boten** *boats*   **vuren** *fires*

When you want to make **man** plural you clearly can't just add **-en** because then you'd get **manen** (*moons*). There is a simple solution: double the end consonant, so the first one goes with the first syllable, thereby keeping it closed.

man *man*   **lek** *leak*   **bot** *bone*   **kus** *kiss*
mannen *men*   **lekken** *leaks*   **botten** *bones*   **kussen** *kisses*

Introductions and talking to and about people

You can introduce someone by saying **Dit is …** and giving his/her name. When referring to them again, you can say **hij** (*he*) if it's a man and **zij** (*she*) if it's a woman.

Here is a complete list of personal (subject) pronouns:

Stressed	Unstressed	Pronouns
SINGULAR		
ik	('k)	*I*
jij	je	*you* (informal)
u	—	*you* (formal)
hij	(ie)	*he*
zij	ze	*she*
het	('t)	*it*
PLURAL		
wij	we	*we*
jullie	—	*you* (informal)
u	—	*you* (formal)
zij	ze	*they*

Most of the pronouns have a stressed and an unstressed form. Generally, the unstressed forms are used, unless you want to emphasize who you're talking about.

There are two ways of addressing someone directly in Dutch. You use **je** or **jij** when you know someone well and you are on a first-name basis. You use **u** to be more polite, or when you don't know someone.

Many verbs change their form according to a rule. These are known as regular verbs. Look at the following table:

helpen *to help*	
ik help	*I help*
jij helpt	*you help* (singular, informal)
u helpt	*you help* (singular, formal)
hij/zij/het helpt	*he/she/it helps*
wij helpen	*we help*
jullie helpen	*you help* (plural, informal)
u helpt	*you help* (plural, formal)
zij helpen	*they help*

However, a few verbs do not follow any logical pattern, including **zijn** (*to be*) and **hebben** (*to have*).

The verb form for **ik** is called the stem of the verb. For the other persons in the singular we use the stem **+ t** : **Ik woon**, **jij woont**, **hij woont**, etc. In the plural, the full form of the verb, the infinitive, is used: **Wij wonen**, **jullie wonen**, **zij wonen**.

The **-t** drops off the end of the verb when asking a question (or when **je/ jij** comes after the verb). This only happens with **je** and **jij** – in all other cases the verb form does not change.

Hoe gaat he t? is a common way of asking after someone's well-being. **Alles goed?** is more informal. To greet someone with **goedemorgen/ middag** is quite formal. People will frequently say simply **dag**, or even more informally (particularly young people) **hoi**.

These are the object pronouns:

mij	*me*	**ons**	*us*
jou/u	*you*	**jullie/u**	*you*
hem/haar	*him/her*	**hen/hun/ze**	*them*

Negative answers

When you want to respond to a question in the negative, you need to add **niet** (*not*) to the sentence.

Werk je?	*Are you working?*
Nee, ik werk niet.	*No, I'm not working.*

Niet often comes at the end of the sentence, but before a preposition.

Nee, ik woon niet in Amsterdam. *No, I don't live in Amsterdam.*

Niet also precedes descriptive words:

Nee, mijn schoenen zijn niet nieuw. *No, my shoes are not new.*

Geen means *no/not any*. In Dutch, you don't say *I do not have a book*, you say *I have no book*.

Ik heb een boek.	**Ik heb geen boek.**

But:

Ik heb het boek.	**Ik heb het boek niet.**

Goodbye

When saying goodbye to someone, you often refer to the time when you will see one another again.

Tot dan.	*See you then (later).*
Tot vanavond.	*See you this evening.*
Tot morgen.	*See you tomorrow.*
Tot volgende week.	*See you next week.*

De, het, een

Names of things (nouns) are often preceded by the words **de** or **het**. For instance, **de appel**, **het beroep**, **het fruit**. These are the Dutch words for *the*.

The word **een** means *one*, but it is also used in Dutch to mean *a/an*.

There are three ways of making words plural. To most words, you add **-en** or **-s** to words ending in **-a, -i, -o, -u, -y** you add **'s**. All plural words are **de** words.

Possession

Here are all the possessive pronouns in Dutch:

Stressed	Unstressed	Pronouns
SINGULAR		
mijn	(m'n)	*my*
jouw	je	*your* (informal)
uw	—	*your* (formal)
zijn	(z'n)	*his*
haar	(d'r)	*her*
PLURAL		
ons/onze	—	*our*
jullie	je	*your* (informal)
uw	—	*your* (formal)
hun	—	*their*

The two forms for *our*, **ons** and **onze**, mean exactly the same thing, except that **ons** is used in front of **het** words and **onze** is used in front of **de** words.

More than one verb

When you use two verbs in the same sentence, the first one, the main or finite verb, comes either at the start of the sentence in a question or as the second item in other sentences. The second verb comes right at the end. This verb at the end does not change its form and is called the infinitive or full verb.

Ik moet morgen hard werken.   *I have to work hard tomorrow.*

The most common verbs to be combined with an infinitive are the modal verbs: **zullen** (*shall*), **mogen** (*may*), **moeten** (*must*), **kunnen** (*can*) and **willen** (*want*).

There is a group of verbs that can be used together with an infinitive (the full verb), but in these cases **te** has to be inserted before the infinitive. Examples of these verbs are:

hoeven	*have to*
proberen	*try*
vergeten	*forget*

The construction **om** + **te** + infinitive is used to express a purpose. It could be translated as *in order to* (although often you would simply translate it as *to*).

Ik ga naar de supermarkt om boodschappen te doen.

Word order

A statement can begin with a word other than the subject. Often expressions of time, e.g. **morgen** or **zaterdag**, occupy this place in the sentence. When this happens, the verb remains in second position and the subject comes straight after the verb.

Ik ga donderdagmiddag …

Donderdagmiddag ga ik …

Deze/Die + dit/dat

Deze/Die and **dit/dat** are the Dutch words for *this/that*. **Deze** (*this*) and **die** (*that*) are used with **de** words. **Dit** (*this*) and **dat** (*that*) are used with **het** words:

| de auto | *the car* | deze auto | *this car* | die auto | *that car* |
| het huis | *the house* | dit huis | *this house* | dat huis | *that house* |

Adjectives

Adjectives such as **oud**, **nieuw**, **kort**, **strak**, etc. sometimes have an **-e** at the end and sometimes they don't.

de jas is oud	de zwarte broek
het blauwe overhemd	*the blue shirt*
een zwarte rugzak	*a black rucksack*

No **-e** is added when the descriptive word comes after the thing it describes. Add **-e** if the description comes before the thing it describes. There is a snag, though. The **-e** is occasionally left out when the descriptive word refers to a **het** word (**het T-shirt**, **het pak**) but is used with **een**, not **het**:

| een dun T-shirt | *a thin T-shirt* |

Big, bigger, biggest

Comparatives (words like *bigger*) and superlatives (words like *biggest*) are used to compare objects, people and ideas or to indicate that they surpass all others. You add **-er** to adjectives to make comparatives, and **-st** to make superlatives. With superlatives you always use **het**:

Adjective	Comparative (add -er)	Superlative (add -st)
mooi	**mooier**	**het mooist**
beautiful	*more beautiful*	*the most beautiful*

Present and past

The present tense can be used to talk about things or events which started in the past and continue in the present. You must use the present tense in combination with **al** (lit. *already*) or **pas** (lit. *only*).

| **Ik woon al drie jaar in Amsterdam.** | *I've lived/been living in Amsterdam for three years.* |

TALKING ABOUT THE PAST

The perfect tense is used to talk about the past. It consists of a form of the verb **hebben** or **zijn** and a past participle.

Ik heb gewandeld.   *I have walked.*

Most verbs in Dutch are regular and form their past participle as follows:

1 Find the stem of the verb.
2 Add **ge-** at the beginning of the stem.
3 Add a **-t** or a **-d** at the end of the stem (a **-t** if the last letter of the stem is a letter in the words 'soft ketchup', otherwise a **-d**).

Most verbs use a form of **hebben** in the perfect tense. A small number of irregular verbs use a form of **zijn** in the perfect tense – those verbs normally indicate a change of place or state:

Hij is met de trein gekomen.   *He has come by train.* (change
                                          of place)

The imperfect tense is also used to talk about the past, and consists of only one verb form: the stem of the verb + **-de(n)** or **-te(n)**. You add **-te** or **-ten** if the last letter of the stem appears in the words 'soft ketchup'. Otherwise you add **-de** or **-den**. The **-n** is added for plural forms.

Infinitive	Stem	Imperfect (SINGULAR)	Imperfect (PLURAL)
werken *work*	**werk**	**werkte**	**werkten**
wonen *live*	**woon**	**woonde**	**woonden**

The imperfect is used when you give extra information about events in the past, after you have already introduced whatever topic you are talking about with the present perfect:

Ik heb twee jaar in Den Bosch   *I lived in Den Bosch for two years.*
gewoond. Ik woonde daar in een   *I lived in a large house there.*
groot huis.

The imperfect is also used to describe things or events that took place regularly in the past.

Separable verbs

Verbs where the first part can be split from the main part are called separable verbs. When you use these verbs as the finite verb in the sentence, the first part splits away and appears at the end of the sentence. For example:

afzeggen	*to cancel*
Hij zegt onze afspraak voor morgen af.	*He's cancelling our appointment for tomorrow.*

When the separable verb is used with another verb, such as **zullen** or **willen**, then it goes to the end of the sentence. The main part of the separable verb meets up with its first part at the end of the sentence. For example:

aankomen	*to arrive*
Ik zal om half zes aankomen.	*I'll arrive at half past five.*

Relative clauses

Relative clauses give extra information about a thing or a person.

De tuin die we hadden, was enorm.	*The garden we had was enormous.*

Relative clauses start either with the relative pronoun **die** or **dat**, depending on the word they refer to. If the relative clause gives information about a **de** word, then you start with **die**; if the relative clause gives information about a **het** word, you start with **dat**. The other important thing to remember is that the verb(s) in a relative clause go(es) to the end of the clause.

If you refer to people in a relative clause and use a preposition, you refer to the person you are talking about as **wie**:

De man met wie ik samenwerk.	*The man with whom I work.*

If you refer to a thing or idea in a relative clause and use a preposition, you refer to the thing you are talking about as **waar**:

De zaak waarover we hebben gesproken.	*The matter we talked about.*

Diminutives

Words which end in **-je** often indicate something is small. This form (a diminutive) is similar to the English -*let* as in *piglet* or *booklet*, but it is used much more frequently in Dutch.

Zullen we op een terrasje een biertje gaan drinken?	*Shall we have a beer on a terrace?*

Zou

You can use **zou/zouden** to ask for something politely or nicely. Because the use of the verb **zou/zouden** is polite in itself, you need not use **alstublieft** in the same sentence:

Zou je dit voor me kunnen doen? *Could you do this for me, please?*

The second meaning of **zou/zouden** is to state or remind someone of what the plan was:

Je zou nog bellen. *You were going to phone.*

Thirdly, **zou/zouden** has the meaning of giving advice:

Je zou wat vroeger naar bed moeten gaan. *You should go to bed a little earlier.*

The fourth function of **zou/zouden** is called the conditional – to show that you, or someone else, would like to do something, if only the conditions were right:

Als ik de loterij zou winnen, zou ik stoppen met werken. *Were I to win the lottery, I would give up work.*

Er + prepositions

You cannot use an object pronoun in combination with a preposition when you refer to a thing. In that case you need to use **er**:

Heb je van het feest gehoord? *Did you hear about the party?*

Ja, ik heb ervan gehoord. *Yes I have (heard about it).*

You don't use **er** when talking about people.

Sub-clauses

In sub-clauses:

▶ the main verb moves to the end of the sub-clause;
▶ the sub-clause always starts with a linking word called a subordinating conjunction.

Dat betekent dat ieder mens anders reageert. *That means that every person responds differently.*

Sub-clauses are linked to main clauses by subordinating conjunctions. Examples are: **als** *when* (at that time), **toen** *when* (in the past), **hoewel** *although*, **omdat** *because*, **als** *if* (in case of).

Pronunciation and spelling

It is important to get your pronunciation right from the start. Here are a few suggestions about how to do this:

▶ Listen to the pronunciation guide on the audio and try to imitate the sounds and words as often as you can. If you do not have the audio, then follow the written instructions very carefully.

▶ When you start work on the units, listen to the dialogues as often as possible and repeat them out loud until your pronunciation comes as close as possible to that of the speaker on the audio.

▶ Record your own voice and then check that it sounds similar to the version on the audio. If you know a native speaker, ask them to correct your pronunciation.

▶ Listen to Dutch native speakers, the Dutch radio and television and even Dutch songs to familiarize yourself with Dutch sounds.

▶ Fortunately, you don't have to worry too much about the stress in words since this generally falls on the first syllable.

▶ Keep going: with practice you will develop a reasonable accent so that you can be easily understood.

Dutch sounds

 00.01

CONSONANTS

As a speaker of English, you won't find Dutch consonants much of a problem. The consonants are generally pronounced the same as in English. Here are the main exceptions:

ch	**licht** *light*	As in Scottish *loch*. You should feel it at the back of your mouth. Sounds softer the further south you go.
g	**gek** *mad*	The same guttural sound as **ch** above. Never pronounced as either English *g* sound.
j	**ja** *yes*	As in English *y* in *yes*.

k, **p**, **t**	**kat** cat, **pop** doll, **tas** bag	The same as in English but without exhaling as much air (hold your hand in front of your mouth and make sure you feel no air coming out with the Dutch words).
r	**rood** red	Can be made by trilling your tongue against the back of your upper teeth or by making friction at the back of the mouth (like a French r).
sch	school school	A combination of **s** and **ch**.
v	**vis** fish	Like English v in give, but sometimes closer to English f, especially at the beginning of words.
w	**wit** white	Between English v and w. Hold your upper teeth against your lower lip.

VOWELS

Dutch vowel sounds can be a bit trickier than the consonants because they differ considerably from those in English. There are short vowel sounds, long vowel sounds and combinations of vowels.

Short vowel sounds

a	**man** man	As in hard but shorter.
e	**lek** leak	As in set but shorter.
i	**lip** lip	As in bit but shorter.
o	**bot** bone	As in hot but shorter.
u	**kus** kiss	Similar to dirt but shorter.

Long vowel sounds

aa	**maan** moon	As in cat but longer.
ee	**leek** layman	As in lane.
eu	**neus** nose	There is no equivalent in English. Try making a vowel sound as in dirt while rounding/pouting your lips tightly.
ie	**niet** not	As in cheat.
oe	**boek** book	As in book but with your lips more rounded.
oo	**boot** boat	As in boat.
uu	**vuur** fire	No equivalent in English. Try making a vowel sound as in leak while pursing your lips. Before r, vowel sounds become much longer.

Combinations of vowels

au/ou	**blauw** *blue*	No equivalent in English. Try making a vowel sound as in *shout* but start by rounding your lips more with your mouth wide open.
aai	**saai** *boring*	A combination of **aa** and **ie**.
eeuw	**eeuw** *century*	A combination of **ee** and **oe**.
ei/ij	**trein** *train*	No equivalent in English. In between the English vowel sounds in *night* and *late*. NB When writing, **ij** is usually written as one letter, like an English *y* with dots.
ieuw	**nieuw** *new*	A combination of **ie** and **oe**.
oei	**doei** *bye*	A combination of **oe** and **ie**.
ooi	**mooi** *beautiful*	A combination of **oo** and **ie**.
ui	**huis** *house*	No equivalent in English. Try making the English vowel sound as in *house* while tightly pursing your lips and pressing your tongue down.
uw	**ruw** *rough*	A combination of **uu** and **oe**.

There is one other Dutch vowel sound which is similar to the English vowel sound in *sister*. This sound (easy to pronounce – just let air escape through your open mouth) can be spelt in different ways:

e	as in **de** *the*
ee	as in **een** *a/an*
i	as in **aardig** *nice*
ij	as in **lelijk** *ugly*

Spelling

Dutch spelling is pretty straightforward and regularized. There is only one major rule to learn, which concerns the vowel sounds **a**, **e**, **o**, **u**.

In the section on short vowel sounds we saw:

man *man*   **lek** *leak*   **bot** *bone*   **kus** *kiss*

These short vowel sounds are always spelt with one letter and always occur in a closed syllable (a syllable ending in a consonant).

In the section on long vowel sounds we saw:

maan *moon*   **leek** *layman*   **boot** *boat*   **vuur** *fire*

These long vowel sounds can be spelt either with two letters (as in the examples) or one letter (**a**, **e**, **o**, **u**), depending on whether they appear in a closed syllable (ending in a consonant) or an open syllable (ending in a vowel).

The long vowel sounds are always spelt with two letters in closed syllables, as in the examples just seen. However, when they appear in an open syllable, they are spelt with a single letter. This happens, for instance, when **-en** is added to make words plural:

maan *moon*	**leek** *layman*	**boot** *boat*	**vuur** *fire*
manen *moons*	**leken** *laymen*	**boten** *boats*	**vuren** *fires*

When **-en** is added, the first syllable becomes an open syllable (the **n**, **k**, **t**, **r** in the middle of the examples becomes part of the second syllable), which means the long vowel sound is spelt with one letter only.

This seems easy enough, although you may well wonder what to do if you want to make **man** *man* plural (you clearly can't just add **-en** because then you'd get **manen** *moons*). There is a simple solution: double the consonant, so the first one goes with the first syllable, thereby keeping it closed.

man *man*	**lek** *leak*	**bot** *bone*	**kus** *kiss*
mannen *men*	**lekken** *leaks*	**botten** *bones*	**kussen** *kisses*

1

Ik ben verpleegster
I am a nurse

In this unit you will learn how to:
▶ *introduce others.*
▶ *name some professions.*
▶ *talk about yourself.*
▶ *provide others with information.*

CEFR: (A1) *Can make social contact by using everyday polite forms of introductions; can say where s/he lives and what languages s/he speaks.*

Formal and informal

There are two ways of addressing someone directly in Dutch. You use **je** or **jij** when you know someone well and you are on a first-name basis. You use **u** to be more polite, or when you don't know someone.

Children and young people are always addressed with **je** or **jij**. Another formal and polite way of addressing people is to use the titles **meneer** (*Mr*) and **mevrouw** (*Mrs, Ms* or *Miss*). However, there is an increasing trend to more informality and more and more people address other adults, even strangers, with **je** or **jij**.

Is it only children who are addressed as **je** or **jij** in Dutch?

Vocabulary builder

01.01 **Listen to the new words and expressions and fill in the missing English meanings.**

INTRODUCING OTHER PEOPLE

Dit is Karel Bos.	*This is Karel Bos.*
Hij spreekt Nederlands en Engels.	*He speaks Dutch and English.*
Hij woont in Amsterdam.	*He lives in Amsterdam.*
Zij is bankassistente.	*She's a bank employee.*
Zij spreekt Duits.	*She speaks German.*
Zij gaat naar de universiteit.	*She goes to university.*

TALKING ABOUT YOURSELF

Ik ben Sara Bakker.	*I'm Sara Bakker.*
Ik ben verpleegster.	*I am a nurse.*
Ik werk in een ziekenhuis.	*I work in a hospital.*
Ik ben student.	*I'm a student.*
Ik werk bij een winkel.	*I work in a shop.*

BEROEPEN *PROFESSIONS*

de kunstenaar (m), de kunstenares (f)	*artist*
de winkelassistent (m), de winkelassistente (f)	*shop assistant*
de zakenman, de zakenvrouw	*businessman/woman*
de website ontwerper (m), ontwerpster (f)	*website designer*

TALEN *LANGUAGES*

Frans	*French*
Duits	_____
Nederlands	_____
Italiaans	_____
Spaans	*Spanish*
Engels	*English*
Russisch	*Russian*
Japans	*Japanese*

1 **If zakenvrouw is the word for** *businesswoman*, **what is the word for** *woman*? **Is it** man, ontwerper, **or** vrouw?

2 **How would you say** *I speak Dutch*?

Text

The following short biographies are written for a Dutch language course website. They give some information about some of the volunteers who help people with their course outside the class.

Dit is Karel Bos.	*This is Karel Bos.*
Hij is zakenman.	*He is a businessman.*
Hij spreekt Engels en Frans.	*He speaks English and French.*
Hij woont in Amsterdam.	*He lives in Amsterdam.*
Hij helpt Jill Johnson.	*He helps Jill Johnson.*

1 **Compare** hij is zakenman **with the English** *he's a businessman*. **What difference do you notice? How would you say** *he's a teacher*?

Dit is Wieteke Jansma.	*This is Wieteke Jansma.*
Zij is kunstenares.	*She is an artist.*
Zij spreekt Engels en Duits.	*She speaks English and German.*

| **Zij woont in Arnhem.** | *She lives in Arnhem.* |
| **Zij helpt Farah Ahmeti.** | *She helps Farah Ahmeti.* |

Look at the patterns of these sentences. You can introduce someone by saying **Dit is** and giving his/her name. In the examples you have **Karel Bos** (a man) and **Wieteke Jansma** (a woman). Then in the examples more information about these people is given. To refer to these people again, you can say **hij** (*he*) if it's a man and **zij** (*she*) if it's a woman.

2 **So how would you say:** *She speaks Dutch; he speaks German?*

3 **Look at the following forms, which give you information about two people. Write a memo about these two people using the same pattern as in the Tekst.**

V

de naam	*name*
het beroep	*job, profession*
de taal	*language*
de woonplaats	*place of residence*
de docent	*teacher*
de bankassistente	*bank employee* (f)
Spaans	*Spanish*
Italiaans	*Italian*

a

Naam:	Tom Peters
Beroep:	docent
Talen:	Engels en Spaans
Woonplaats:	Utrecht
Helpt:	Allie Mitchell

b

Naam:	Leona Beke
Beroep:	bankassistent
Talen:	Engels en Italiaans
Woonplaats:	Amersfoort
Helpt:	Marisa Delporte

Language discovery

You have now learnt how to talk about someone else using **hij** or **zij**. But if you want to talk about yourself you use the pronoun **ik** (*I*) and you will need to change the form of the verb:

Ik ben Sara Bakker.	**Ik woon in Hilversum.**
Ik ben verpleegster.	**Ik help Ben Mendoza.**
Ik spreek Engels en Frans.	**Ik werk in een ziekenhuis.**

1 **Introduce yourself using the pattern given earlier as if you were Karel Bos. Then try it as if you were Tom Peters.**

2 **Write two short introductions for yourself for the website mentioned in the Tekst as if you were the following people.**

   a *naam:* Gail Boonstra; beroep: computerprogrammeur; talen: Nederlands (Dutch) en Engels; woonplaats: Edam; werk: bij een bedrijf (with a company)

   b *naam:* Ad Visser; beroep: manager; talen: alleen (only) Nederlands; woonplaats: Zutphen; werk: bij/in een winkel (in a shop)

> **LANGUAGE TIP**
> Note the different preposition **bij**. There are no clear rules as to when to use what preposition.

SAYING *YOU*...

If you want to address someone, you use the pronoun **jij** (*you*) and use the verbs in the form as shown:

Jij bent Marco Cohen.

Jij bent tandarts.

Jij spreekt Engels and Russisch.

Jij woont in Leeuwarden.

Jij werkt thuis.

REGULAR VERBS

From all the texts so far, you can tell that you have to change the form of the verb depending on who or what you're speaking about. Many verbs change their form according to a rule. These are known as regular verbs. Look at the following table.

helpen	to help
ik help	I help
jij helpt	you help (singular, informal)
u helpt	you help (singular, formal)
hij/zij/het helpt	he/she/it helps
wij helpen	we help
jullie helpen	you help (plural, informal)
u helpt	you help (plural, formal)
zij helpen	they help

3 What word in the table means *it*? What about *she* and *they*?

PLURAL

The grammatical term for talking about more than one person is 'plural'. In Dutch the plural form of the verb is always the whole verb:

wij/jullie/zij helpen	*we/you/they are helping/help*
wij/jullie/zij wonen	*we/you/they are living/live*
wij/jullie/zij spreken	*we/you/they are speaking/speak*
wij/jullie/zij werken	*we/you/they are working/work*

4 Complete the verbs denken (*to think*) and drinken (*to drink*) following the pattern given for helpen.

denken *to help*		**drinken** *to drink*	
Ik _____		**ik** _____	
jij helpt		**jij** _____	
u _____		_____ **drinkt**	
hij/zij/het		**hij/zij/het** _____	
wij _____		**wij** _____	
jullie _____		**jullie** _____	
u _____		**u** _____	
zij _____		**zij** _____	

5 Look at endings of the u forms of the verb in the singular and plural. What do you notice?

TWO IRREGULAR VERBS

Most verbs follow the same pattern. However, a few verbs do not follow any logical pattern, including **zijn** (*to be*) and **hebben** (*to have*):

zijn	to be
ik ben	I am
jij bent	you are (singular, informal)
u bent	you are (singular, formal)
hij/zij/het is	he/she/it is
wij zijn	we are
jullie zijn	you are (plural, informal)
u bent	you are (plural, formal)
zij zijn	they are

hebben	to have
ik heb	I have
jij hebt/heeft	you have (singular, informal)
u hebt/heeft	you have (singular, formal)
hij/zij/het heeft	he/she/it has
wij hebben	we have
jullie hebben	you have (plural, informal)
u hebt	you have (plural, formal)
zij hebben	they have

Ik heb een beroep.   I have a job.

Zij hebben een avondwinkel.   They have a late-night shop.

U hebt een kind.   You (formal) have a child.

Listen and speak

01.02 Here is a list of people you are going to speak to at a party. Go up to them and check who they are, using the correct form of address (e.g. u or jij). For example:

> **Meneer Verkerk**   U bent meneer Verkerk?
> **Jos Woudstra**   Jij bent Jos Woudstra?

de winkelbediende   shop assistant

de medestudent   fellow student

het kind   child

  a Mevrouw Schipper (een winkelbediende)
  b Wim Den Uyl (een medestudent)
  c Joop Tersteeg (een kind)
  d Meneer Brink (een docent)

> **VOCABULARY TIP**
> **schilderen**   to paint

Dialogue

01.03 **Read and listen to the following dialogue which takes place at the introduction session of a residential course. The participants recognize one another from the participant list.**

Mia	Jij bent Mieke, hè?
Mieke	Ja, en jij bent Rianne?
Mia	Nee, ik ben Mia.
Mieke	O ja. Jij schildert toch?
Mia	Ja, ik ben kunstenares.

Note that Mieke and Mia use the words **hè** and **toch** to indicate they aren't certain. This is like saying *aren't you?* or *don't you?* in English.

Practice 1

1 **You are meeting the people who work as volunteers for your agency and you want to check that the information on your files is correct. Check with Sara Bakker and Leona Beke, about whom you have already had information in this unit, that the information you have is correct. You can do this by asking them a question based on the following pattern:**

Jij bent tandarts, hè?   *You are a dentist, aren't you?*

U spreekt toch Spaans?   *You speak Spanish, don't you?*

2 **You are collecting data about people for your particular organization. Using the information given, write down the appropriate information for your files. Example sentences could be:**

Peter van Dam woont in Den Haag.

Meneer Verkerk en Jos Woudstra wonen in Haarlem.

  a **Mevrouw Schipper, Amersfoort**
  b **Meneer Brink, Utrecht**
  c **Joop Tersteeg, Leeuwarden**
  d **Marco Cohen, Leeuwarden**

3 Next you want to file information about the languages people speak. Using the information about people already given in this unit plus the extra information given, write down the appropriate sentences. For example:

Kees Spier spreekt Frans en Italiaans.

Klaas Kortemans, Karel Bos en Sara Bakker spreken Engels en Frans.

   a Saskia de Boer, Engels en Duits
   b Ruud Krol, Engels en Spaans
   c Sietske Zwart, Engels en Russisch
   d Marco Cohen, Engels en Russisch

Go further

BEROEPEN JOBS

1 01.04 In Dutch the female version of a profession occasionally has a different form. Listen and complete the table with the missing English meanings. Then repeat after the native speaker, paying attention to your pronunciation:

man	vrouw	
docent	docente	*teacher*
winkelassistent	winkelassistente	*shop assistant* _____
tandarts	tandarts	*dentist*
zakenman	zakenvrouw	*businessperson*
manager	manager	*manager*
bankassistent	bankassistente	*bank assistant*
verkoper	verkoopster	*salesperson*
verpleger	verpleegster	_____
student	studente	_____
website-ontwerper	website-ontwerpster	*website designer*
administrateur	administratrice	_____
architect	architect	_____
acteur	actrice	*actor (actress)*

To indicate that people, jobs or animals are female, the following endings are often used:

▶ add **-e**: **assistent**, **assistente** (*assistant*)
▶ add **-es**: **zanger**, **zangeres** (*singer*)
▶ add **-in**: **boer**, **boerin** (*farmer*)
▶ change **-er** into **-ster**: **ontwerper**, **ontwerpster** (*designer*)

Practice 2

1 01.05 Wat doet hij/zij? *What does he/she do for a living?* **Listen to the description on the audio (or read the following) and find the correct answers. For example:**

Hij werkt op een school. (*He works in a school.*)

Antwoord (*Answer*): **Hij is docent.**

- **a** Hij werkt in een winkel.
- **b** Hij trekt tanden. (*He pulls teeth.*)
- **c** Zij gaat naar de universiteit. (*She goes to university.*)
- **d** Zij schildert.
- **e** Hij ontwerpt websites.
- **f** Zij werkt op een bank.
- **g** Hij ontwerpt huizen en gebouwen. (*He designs houses and buildings.*)
- **h** Zij doet administratief werk. (*She does administrative work.*)
- **i** Hij speelt in een film. (*He is in a film.*)

2 01.06 **To test your knowledge of the Netherlands and Flanders, listen to the audio and try to match these statements with places on the map.**

a The capital of the Netherlands.

b In this part of Belgium people speak Dutch.

c Tourists know this town particularly for its cheese market.

d Not the capital of the Netherlands, but the seat of the Dutch government.

e Not only the European capital, also the seat of the Belgian government.

f This ancient Roman town has strong modern European connections.

g Known for the famous landing of English and Canadian parachutists in 1944.

h The city where the famous 17th-century painter Frans Hals lived and worked.

i The sea which is a protected natural area.

j A thriving cultural city which is also one of the biggest ports in the world.

k This thriving old cultural centre south of the Netherlands also has a very big port.

l This is the centre of the Dutch TV industry.

m This city in the north has long been ignored by tourists and Dutch alike, but it's up and coming and you can't miss seeing its famous new museum.

de Noordzee

de Waddenzee

Groningen

Leeuwarden

Alkmaar

IJsselmeer

Amsterdam

Haarlem

Hilversum

Amersfoort

Utrecht

NEDERLAND

Den Haag

IJssel

Rotterdam

Lek

Nederrijn

Arnhem

Waal

Rijn

Maas

Den Bosch

Eindhoven

Maas

Brugge

Schelde

Antwerpen

Gent

VLAANDEREN

Brussel

Maastricht

BELGIË

Test yourself

1 Give the feminine form of these words (remember that some words have identical forms):
   a de kunstenaar
   b de tandarts
   c de bankassistent
   d hij
   e de acteur
   f de docent

2 Introduce yourself in Dutch by saying:
   a What your name is.
   b In which town you live.
   c Which languages you speak.

3 Translate:
   a Carla and Hatif live in Rotterdam.
   b Ask an elderly gentleman if he is **meneer Bolken**.
   c Ask a friend what Ruud does for a living.
   d Fransisca works in a shop.
   e Peter and Remco help Marisa.
   f Ask mevrouw Simmerink if she speaks German.
   g Nicole is a salesperson (in a shop).

SELF CHECK

I CAN ...

- ○ ... introduce others.
- ○ ... name some professions.
- ○ ... talk about myself.
- ○ ... provide others with information.

2

Waar woont u?
Where do you live?

In this unit you will learn how to:
▶ *greet someone and ask how they are.*
▶ *ask for information about someone.*
▶ *ask for and understand directions.*

CEFR: (A1) *Can understand questions and instructions addressed carefully and slowly to him/her and follow short, simple directions.*

Greetings

Hoe gaat het? is a common way of asking after someone's well-being. **Alles goed?** is more informal and used by people who know one another relatively well. To greet someone with **goedemorgen/middag** is quite formal. People will frequently say simply **dag**, or even more informally (particularly young people) **hoi**.

In a relatively formal situation you are more likely to answer positively to the question **hoe gaat 't?**, although, on the whole, Dutch people tend to be quite straightforward and direct and will not hesitate to respond with a negative answer.

In a formal situation it is polite to thank someone for the query after your well-being with **dank u** *thank you*. The expressions **'t gaat wel** and **'t gaat, 't gaat** both mean *I'm OK-ish*, but the latter expression is more informal.

How do young people typically greet each other in Dutch? Do they say **Hoe gaat het?**, **Alles goed?**, or **Hoi?**

V Vocabulary builder

02.01 Try and fill in the blank words.

hoi	*hello*
dag	*hello*
goedemorgen	*good morning*
goedemiddag	_____
goedenavond	*good evening*
uw	*your* (formal)
je	*your* (informal)
heten	*to be called*
brengen	*to bring/take*
zitten (here)	*to live*
in het buitenland	*abroad*
doen	*to do*
Wat doe jij?	_____
wat leuk	*that's nice/oh, how nice*
ziek	*ill*
ik ben jarig	*it's my birthday*
morgen	*tomorrow*
het schilderij	*painting*
het huis	*house*

Dialogue 1

On her first day at school, Ines meets her teacher for the first time.

02.02 Listen to the conversation. What does Ines ask Rosie?

Juf Rosie	Dag. Hoe heet jij?
Ines	Ik heet Ines. Hoe heet jij?
Juf Rosie	Ik heet juf Rosie.

> **LANGUAGE TIP**
>
> At many primary schools in the Netherlands children address their teachers with **je** or **jij** and call them by their first name preceded by **juf** in the case of female teachers, and by **meester** in the case of male teachers. Even the head of school is addressed in this manner. In Belgium, the relationship between teachers and children tends to be more formal.

New expressions 1

The expression for asking how someone is needs to be learnt because it is completely different from the English. There are different ways of answering this question:

(Het gaat) uitstekend   (Het gaat) goed,   (Ach, het) gaat wel   (Het gaat) niet zo goed
                  prima   't gaat, 't gaat   't kan beter

Hoe gaat het?

(Het gaat) uitstekend.

(Het gaat) goed, prima.

(Ach, het) gaat wel.

't gaat, 't gaat.

(Het gaat) niet zo goed.

't kan beter.

1 **Read the following situations. Can you tell which is the most formal of the three and why?**

   a Hans meets his friend Jack in a snack bar:

Jack	Hoi Hans. Hoe gaat het?
Hans	't gaat, 't gaat.

   b Nathalie calls her sister Liddie:

Nathalie	Alles goed?
Liddie	Ja, 't gaat wel.

   c Two women meet in a local shop:

Mevrouw Droog	Goedemiddag, mevrouw Pruim.
Mevrouw Pruim	Hoe gaat het met u?
Mevrouw Droog	't Gaat uitstekend. Dank u wel.

18

2 **Give the appropriate greeting for the following people when you meet them in the street. Ask how they are and provide the answer as well. There are various possibilities, but use the pictures as a guide. Think about the level of formality you are likely to use.**

a Mevrouw Dekker

b Your friend Henk

c Jan, a teenager

d Meneer Kok

Dialogue 2

Two friends talk about an acquaintance from an evening class.

02.03 Listen to the conversation and answer the questions.

1 Where does Karel live?

Merel	Waar woont Karel eigenlijk?
Janneke	Hij woont in Haarlem.
Merel	En waar werktie?
Janneke	Hij werkt in Amsterdam.

> **LANGUAGE TIP**
>
> The word **eigenlijk** means *actually*. Merel uses it because otherwise she would sound a little abrupt in asking Janneke where Karel lives.

2 Where does Karel work?

> **LANGUAGE TIP**
>
> When speaking informally, people often say **ie** instead of **hij**. Note that **ie** is not normally used in writing, and **ie** is never used at the beginning of a sentence, where the full form **hij** must be used.

New expressions 2

QUESTIONS

02.04 Listen to these new expressions using question words.

A patient wakes up in a hospital and asks:

Waar ben ik?	*Where am I?*
Je bent in het ziekenhuis!	*You're in hospital!*

Amy has met some people on holiday and asks:

Waar werken jullie?	*Where do you* (plural) *work?*
Wij werken in een kroeg.	*We work in a pub.*

Language discovery 1

ASKING QUESTIONS

Asking an open question using a question word (e.g. *what*, *where*, *how*, etc.) is easy in Dutch. As in English, the question word (in this case **waar**) comes first. This is followed by the verb (the action word), which is then followed by the subject (the person or thing the sentence is about), e.g.:

question word + verb + subject

Waar woont Karel?   *Where does Karel live?*

When you make a simple statement instead of asking a question, the subject often comes before the verb and any other parts of the sentence come after the verb:

subject + verb + other information

Karel woont bij zijn vriend.   *Karel lives with his boy friend.*

Dialogue 3

02.05 **Now listen to the following conversations and answer the questions.**

1 Does Hans live in Wibautstraat?

Jaap	Jij woont toch in de Wibautstraat?
Hans	Nee, in de Blasiusstraat. En waar woon jij?
Jaap	In de Houtstraat.

2 What does Jans do in Utrecht?

Jans	Jij werkt in Rotterdam, hè?
Ella	Nee, in Den Haag. En waar werk jij?
Jans	In Utrecht.

Language discovery 2

WONEN AND WERKEN

Look at the verbs **wonen** and **werken**. The **t** drops off the end of the verb when asking a question (or when **je/jij** comes after the verb). This only happens with **je** and **jij**. In all other cases the verb form does not change. However:

Waar zit jij?	*Where do you sit?/Where are you?*
Waar eet jij?	*Where do you eat?/Where do you normally eat?*

Note that the spelling of **zitten** and **eten** changes. Look at the spelling rules.

1 **Make up a dialogue along the following pattern, using the information given. Make sure you use the correct forms:** hij, zij, ik, jullie **or** jij. **For example:**

Ask Mieke where Ellie lives.
– Mieke, waar woont Ellie eigenlijk?
– Zij woont in de Turfstraat.
Ask Mieke where she works.
– Waar werk jij?
– Ik werk in Den Haag.

  a Ask Frans where he lives.
  b Ask Ellie where Frans and Mieke live.
  c Ask Mieke where Janneke lives.
  d Ask Ellie where she works.
  e Ask Frans where Karel works (Amsterdam).
  f Ask Dennis and Ria where they live (Groningen).

MORE QUESTION WORDS

So far, we have looked at questions asking for information about *where* **waar** something is. You can use the same pattern with other question words, such as **wat**.

WAT *WHAT*

Henny is talking to Martine in a bar.

Henny	Wat doe jij?
Martine	Ik ben docente. En jij? Wat doe jij?
Henny	Ik ben verpleegster.

Meneer Schmidt meets Jaap Muller.

Meneer Schmidt	Wat doe jij?
Jaap	Ik ben informatiespecialist. Wat doet u?
Meneer Schmidt	Ik ben directeur van een middelgroot bedrijf.

2 **Ask the following people what they do and give their reply.**
   Use the correct form of address, either u **or** jij.
   a mevrouw Kooimanverpleegster
   b Wim advocaat (*lawyer*)
   c Dirk docent
   d meneer Spaans dokter
   e Jannieredacteur (*editor*)

3 **Look at the following conversation about who will bring what to**
   a picnic party.

Katy	Jij brengt toch een pizza?
Emma	Nee, een quiche. Wat breng jij?
Katy	Een appeltaart.

Now complete the following dialogues in the same pattern.

a	**Hanny**	Jij drinkt toch wijn?
	Marja	Nee, bier. _____?
b	**Peter**	Jij zoekt toch het station?
	Helen	Nee, het postkantoor. _____?
c	**Annie**	Jij maakt toch de soep?
	Raymond	Nee, het slaatje. _____?
d	**Meneer Vogel**	U schrijft toch kinderboeken?
	Mevrouw de Loo	Nee, romans. Wat _____ u?

Dialogue 4

At a family reunion Ellie meets her cousin Hester. They haven't met since they were children. They talk about themselves and about Frans, Hester's brother.

 02.06 Listen to the following conversation. Can you tell where Frans lives?

Ellie	Waar woon je eigenlijk?
Hester	Ik woon in Leiden.
Ellie	En waar woont Frans?
Hester	Oh, Frans zit in het buitenland.
Ellie	Ooh, wat leuk! Wat doet hij daar?
Hester	Hij werkt bij een bank in Londen.

Language discovery 3

Note that the pattern with the word **wat** in Ellie's exclamation **'wat leuk'** can be used to respond to all sorts of situations, e.g.:

Wat koud!	*Oh, it's so cold!*
Wat vervelend!	*What a nuisance!*
Wat interessant!	*That's interesting!*
Wat een mooie film!	*What a beautiful film!*
Wat knap!	*That's very clever!*

There are a few verbs in Dutch which, in addition to their literal meaning, can also mean *to be*. Two of these verbs are **staan** (lit. *to stand*) and **zitten** (lit. *to sit*). The latter can also mean *to live*.

> **LANGUAGE TIP**
> **Staan** is something of an irregular verb: **ik sta**, **jij staat**, **hij/zij staat**.

To some degree you need to acquire a feeling for when to use **staan** or **zitten**, but you sound quite authentic when you use these verbs correctly, so it's worth the effort. It might help you if you think about the literal meaning of these verbs as 'standing' and 'sitting':

De suiker staat op tafel.	*The sugar is on the table.*
De melk staat in de koelkast.	*The milk is in the fridge.*
Ik sta in een telefooncel.	*I'm in a phone box.*
Ik zit in de gevangenis.	*I'm in prison.*

1 Ask where the following are:
   a Ask in a restaurant where the toilet is (**de w.c.**).
   b Making coffee at a friend's house, ask where the coffee is
        (**de koffie**).
   c Ask where Lieve lives (do not use the verb **wonen**).
   d Looking for a child who is hiding, call out and ask where s/he is (do
        not use the verb *to be*).

GIVING DIRECTIONS

aan de linkerkant aan je linkerhand linksaf

links

rechtdoor

aan de rechterkant aan je rechterhand rechtsaf

rechts

Dialogue 5

Karin and Saskia have a discussion about where Naimal lives.

Answer the questions.

1 Where does Naimal live?

Karin	Waar woont Naimal?
Saskia	In de laan van Osnabrück.
Karin	Waar is dat?
Saskia	Hier rechtdoor, dan links.

2 How do you get there?

Dialogue 6

How do you get to the supermarket? Do you go left or right?

Jaap	Dag mevrouw, ik zoek een supermarkt.
Mevrouw	Er is een Albert Heijn vlakbij.
Visser	Je gaat hier linksaf, langs het postkantoor. Het is aan de rechterkant.
Jaap	Dank u.

Dialogue 7

Rita asks the barman a question.

Where is the telephone?

Rita	Waar is de telefoon?
Barman	De trap op, aan je linkerhand.
Rita	Bedankt.

> **LANGUAGE TIP**
> When asking for directions, you will often get a very complicated answer. Don't be frustrated if you don't understand everything that is being said. Simply concentrate on the most important directions, which will normally be the words and phrases given in this unit.

Practice

Now practise asking for information about where something is, using the word waar**, and giving simple directions. Identify the signs for the following places and give answers about where they are. For example:**

Waar is het internetcafé? Het internetcafé is aan de rechterkant.

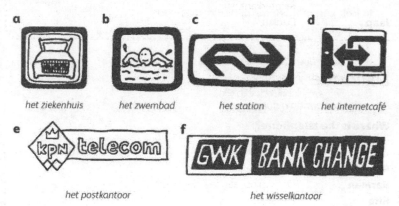

a het ziekenhuis   b het zwembad   c het station   d het internetcafé

het postkantoor   het wisselkantoor

a het ziekenhuis
b het zwembad
c het station
d het internetcafé
e het postkantoor
f het wisselkantoor

Test yourself

1 Ask Frans where Karel works (Amsterdam).

2 Ask Dennis and Ria where they live (Groningen).

3 Your friend is bragging and generally asking for a lot of attention. You respond to all her statements appropriately with an expression from the following list. For example:

Ik heb een nieuwe auto. *I've got a new car.*

Oh, wat leuk!

a Ik ben ziek.

b Ik ben morgen jarig.

c Ik spreek Russisch en Japans.

d Ik heb een schilderij van Picasso.

e Ik heb een huis in Frankrijk.

1 Wat koud!

2 Wat vervelend!

3 Wat interessant!

4 Oh, wat leuk!

5 Wat knap!

SELF CHECK

I CAN ...

... greet someone and ask how they are.

... ask for information about someone.

... ask for directions.

3 In de supermarkt
In the supermarket

In this unit you will learn how to:
- ▶ *go shopping.*
- ▶ *ask prices.*
- ▶ *name several kinds of food.*

CEFR: (A1) *Can understand sentences and frequently used expressions related to areas of shopping.*

Brood en bier   *Bread and beer*

The most common way of starting the day in the Netherlands is with **een boterham** *a slice of bread*, plus **boter** *butter* and **kaas** *cheese*. Cheese can be **jong** *young*, **belegen** *mature* or **oud** *extra mature*. Another popular thing to put on your **boterham** in the Low Countries is **hagelslag**, a kind of 'hundreds and thousands', which is usually made of high quality chocolate (dark, milk or white), but which also comes in various other flavours.

One of the most popular alcoholic drinks in the Netherlands and Belgium is **bier**, also known as **pils** *lager*. As you probably know, there are lots of different varieties of Dutch and Belgian beer, including various types of **witbier** *white beer*. When ordering you can ask for **een bier/pils** or **een biertje/pilsje** (literally, *a small beer*). Beer comes in **een glas** *a glass*, **een flesje** *a bottle*, and, for consumers of large quantities, in **een krat** *a crate*.

Bij de kassa   *At the checkout*

In order to promote recycling of glass, you will have to pay **statiegeld** for some drinks in glass bottles. This is an extra charge on top of the price of the product which you will get back on returning the bottle to the supermarket (the same goes for other shops).

If a crate of beer is 11.10 euros, why would you need to pay 15.1 euros? Is it because of **statiegeld** or **hagelslag**?

Vocabulary builder

Listen to the new words and expressions and fill in the missing English meanings.

hoeveel	*how much/how many*
kosten	_____
graag	*please*
alstublieft (informal: alsjeblieft)	*please*
de winkelbediende	*shop assistant*

HET FRUIT *FRUIT*

de appel de druif	de peer	de perzik de tomaat
de appels	de druiven	de peren de perziken de tomaten

DE KAAS *CHEESE*

jonge kaas
belegen kaas
oude kaas

BROOD *BREAD*

bruin brood
wit brood
het bolletje/puntje

HET BELEG *THINGS TO HAVE ON YOUR BREAD*

de boter

de ham

de pindakaas de hagelslag

1 How would you ask de winkelbediende for some white bread and mature cheese?

BOODSCHAPPEN *DO THE (GROCERY) SHOPPING*

de sinaasappelsap
de jus d'orange

spa blauw
spa rood

de wijn
de rode/witte wijn

de volle melk
de halfvolle melk
de magere melk

2 Look at the items illustrated opposite, choose five items you like and practise asking how much each item costs. For example:

Hoeveel kost een wit brood?

Dialogue 1

Josie is buying cheese.

03.02 Listen to the conversation and answer the questions.

1 How much does a kilo of brie cost?

Josie	Hoeveel kost de brie?
Winkelbediende	6 euro per kilo.
Josie	250 gram brie dan graag.
Winkelbediende	Alstublieft.
Josie	Dank u wel.

2 How much brie does Josie buy?

Language discovery 1

NUMMERS NUMBERS 1–20

03.03

0 **nul**	6 **zes**	12 **twaalf**	18 **achttien**
1 **één**	7 **zeven**	13 **dertien**	19 **negentien**
2 **twee**	8 **acht**	14 **veertien**	20 **twintig**
3 **drie**	9 **negen**	15 **vijftien**	
4 **vier**	10 **tien**	16 **zestien**	
5 **vijf**	11 **elf**	17 **zeventien**	

1 03.04 Listen to the three phone numbers given on the audio and write them down.

2 Read the following numbers out loud in Dutch: 7, 4, 12, 5, 19, 2, 8, 10, 20, 17.

New expressions 1

uw	*your* (formal)
je	*your* (informal)
PINnummer	*personal identification number*

1 **03.05 Answer the following questions using the patterns in these examples:**

Wat is uw huisnummer? (8) (*What is your house number?*)

– Acht.

Wat is je telefoonnummer? (564367) (*What is your telephone number?*)

– Vijf zes vier drie zes zeven.

Wat is je PINnummer? (17 14) (*What is your PIN number?*)

– Één zeven één vier.

   a Wat is uw huisnummer? (17)
   b Wat is je telefoonnummer? (987621)
   c Wat is je PINnummer? (11 19)

2 **Do the following sums and write them down in words.**

> **LANGUAGE TIP**
> + **plus** – **min** × **keer** = **is**

For example: 3 + 2 = **drie plus twee is vijf**

a	2 + 11	**e**	17 – 9 =
b	20 – 8 =	**f**	7 + 6 =
c	4 × 4	**g**	18 – 4 =
d	3 × 5	**h**	6 – 6 =

Language discovery 2

MORE NUMBERS

03.06

20	**twintig**	60	**zestig**
21	**eenentwintig**	70	**zeventig**
22	**tweeëntwintig**	80	**tachtig**
23	**drieëntwintig**	90	**negentig**
24	**vierentwintig**	100	**honderd**
25	**vijfentwintig**	200	**tweehonderd**
26	**zesentwintig**	300	**driehonderd**
27	**zevenentwintig**	128	**honderd achtentwintig**
28	**achtentwintig**	282	**tweehonderd tweeëntachtig**
29	**negenentwintig**	465	**vierhonderd vijfenzestig**
30	**dertig**	746	**zevenhonderd zesenveertig**
40	**veertig**	1000	**duizend**
50	**vijftig**		

A trema (two little dots above a letter) is used for numbers such as **tweeëntwintig**, **drieënzestig**, etc. This is to avoid reading the 'e's as one long sound; 22 should be pronounced as **twee-en-twintig** and 63 as **drie-en-zestig**. Practise these numbers and learn them by heart. You will need to spend some time on this.

1 **Wijnand is taking stock in the supermarket. He is making a list of how many items there are left. Read the list out loud. For example:**

25 potten pindakaas

Er zijn nog vijfentwintig potten pindakaas.

There are (still) 25 jars of peanut butter.

- **a** 32 croissants
- **b** 175 flessen witte wijn
- **c** 239 flessen rode wijn
- **d** 64 pakken melk (*cartons of milk*)
- **e** 95 kuipjes boter (*tubs of butter*)
- **f** 78 tubes tandpasta (*tubes of toothpaste*)
- **g** 116 plastic tasjes (*plastic bags*)
- **h** 22 kratten pils (*crates of beer*)

2 Ask how much the following cost and provide the answers. For example:

Hoeveel kost de fles rode wijn?

De fles rode wijn kost 4 euros 25.

   a Hoeveel kost de krat pils?

   b Hoeveel kost het pak melk?

   c Hoeveel kosten de peren?

   d Hoeveel kost de kaas?

   1 Het pak melk kost 76 (euro) cent.

   2 De kaas kost 3 euro 5 per kilo.

   3 De krat pils kost 11 euro 10.

   4 De peren kosten 1 euro 88 per kilo.

Hoeveel? can be used to ask about both quantity (*how much?*) and number (*how many?*). For example:

Hoeveel flessen wijn heb je?	*How many bottles of wine have you got?*
Hoeveel sinaasappels heb je?	*How many oranges have you got?*
Hoeveel pasta eet hij?	*How much pasta does he eat?*

New expressions 2

HOEVEEL HEB JE NODIG? *HOW MUCH/MANY DO YOU NEED?*

het pak rijst	*packet of rice*
de bonen	*beans*
de druiven	*grapes*
de bloemkool	*cauliflower*

Your partner has written a shopping list and you are checking the items together. Ask him how much is needed of each of the items listed. For example:

Hoeveel flessen wijn heb je nodig?

Ik heb 3 flessen nodig.

Hoeveel tomaten heb je nodig?

Ik heb 1 kilo tomaten nodig.

- **a** sinaasappels (5)
- **b** pakken melk (2)
- **c** flessen bier (12)
- **d** bloemkolen (1)
- **e** appels (1 kilo)
- **f** pakken rijst (4)
- **g** bonen (2 kilo)
- **h** druiven (1 pond)

Language discovery 3

When you say you need something in Dutch what you literally say is *I have apples necessary*: **Ik heb appels nodig**.

Note that in the question **Hoeveel flessen wijn heb je nodig?** the word **je** was used instead of **jij**. The only difference between these forms is that **jij** must be used in situations where *you* is stressed. Whereas in English you would normally change the tone of your voice in these situations, in Dutch you change the unstressed form **je** to the stressed form **jij**. **Je** is the unstressed version of *you*. However, generally you can use either **je** or **jij** if *you* is not emphasized in the sentence. Some of the other pronouns (person words) also have an unstressed version. Look at the following:

Stressed	Unstressed
ik	–
jij	**je** (informal)
u	– (formal)
hij	**ie** (spoken language only)
zij	**ze**
het	**'t**
wij	**we**
jullie	–
u	– (formal)
zij	**ze**

DE, HET *THE*

You may have noticed that names of things (nouns) are often preceded by the words **de** or **het**, e.g. **de appel**, **het beroep**, **het fruit**. These are the Dutch words for *the*. About two-thirds of the words use **de** for *the* and the remaining third of words use **het**. It is generally impossible, unfortunately, to tell from looking at a word whether it is a **de** or **het** word. You will just have to learn these words by heart.

MORE THAN ONE

There are two ways of saying that there are more than one: by adding **-en** or **-s**. The rules for when to add **-en** and when to add **-s** can be quite tricky to learn, so you may prefer simply learning the plural for each word individually as you come across it. However, here are the rules anyway, so you know what we're talking about:

▶ Add **-s** when the word has at least two syllables and ends with **-el**, **-en**, **-em**, **-er**, **-je**.
▶ Add **-'s** when the word ends with **-a**, **-i**, **-o**, **-u**, **-y**.
▶ Add **-en** to all other nouns.

Add -s or -'s		Add -en	
de tafel *table*	de tafels	**het boek** *book*	de boeken
de kamer *room*	de kamers	**het ding** *thing*	de dingen
het meisje *girl*	de meisjes	**de stoel** *chair*	de stoelen
de foto *photo*	de foto's	**de fiets** *bicycle*	de fietsen
de auto *car*	de auto's	**de man** *man*	de mannen
de hobby *hobby*	de hobby's	**de maan** *moon*	de manen
de taxi *taxi*	de taxi's		
de euro *euro*	de euro's		

NB All plurals use **de** for *the*.

Try making plurals for these words:

a appel
b vrouw
c disco
d fles
e programma
f computer
g gracht (*canal*)

New expressions 3

tomatensoep   *tomato soup*

de kaas   *cheese*

sinaasappel   *orange*

Dialogue 2

Jasper and Ine discuss which food they will have.

03.07 Listen to the conversation and answer the questions.

1 Which cheese would Ine like?

Jasper	Welke soep wil je?
Ine	De tomatensoep.
Jasper	En welke wijn wil je?
Ine	Beaujolais, graag.
Jasper	Welke kaas wil je?
Ine	De jonge kaas.
Jasper	Welk fruit wil je?
Ine	Een sinaasappel.

> **LANGUAGE TIP**
> You will see that the question word **welk/welke** has two forms. How do you know
> when to use which?
> The answer is that **welke** is used with **de** words, including plurals, and **welk** is used
> with **het** words. For example:
> **de wijn → welke wijn?**
> **het fruit → welk fruit?**
> **de appels** (plural) → **welke appels?**

2 Ask your partner which one he/she wants.

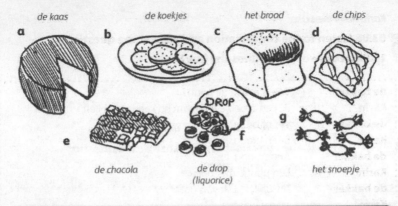

de kaas   de koekjes   het brood   de chips

a   b   c   d

e   f   g

de chocola   de drop (liquorice)   het snoepje

> **LANGUAGE TIP**
> The Dutch use the word **chips** for *crisps* and **patat** for *chips*.

New expressions 4

Wie is er aan de beurt?	*Who is next?*
een broodje met ham en kaas	*a cheese and ham sandwich*
wit/bruin	*white/brown (bread)*
een puntje	*a crusty roll*
Anders nog iets?	*Anything else?*
Dat was het?	*Was that all?*
Dat is dan … bij elkaar.	*That will be … altogether, then.*
tot ziens	*goodbye*

Dialogue 3

Karin visits the baker.

03.08 Listen to the conversation and answer the questions.

1 What type of bread does she buy?

de bakker	Wie is er aan de beurt?
Karin	Ik. Een broodje met ham en kaas, alstublieft.
de bakker	Wit of bruin?
Karin	Bruin brood, graag.
de bakker	Anders nog iets?
Karin	Een puntje met brie.
de bakker	Alstublieft. Dat was het?
Karin	Ja, dat was het.
de bakker	Dat is dan 4,50 euro bij elkaar.
Karin	Alstublieft.
de bakker	Dank u wel.
Karin	Dag.
de bakker	Tot ziens, mevrouw.

2 How much in total is Karin's shopping?

You're going to the supermarket. Make up a boodschappenlijstje
(*shopping list*) **of as many things as you would normally buy in real
life. Use this book as a guide, but you might also want to try and
use a dictionary.**

Once you have your own **boodschappenlijstje** use it to say what you
need or want to buy, using the following structures:

Ik heb ... nodig	*I need ...*
Ik wil ...	*I want ...*

Try and be as specific as possible about how much you need. Here are
some weights and measures:

een gram	*a gram*	**een ons**	*an ounce (100 grams)*
een kilo	*a kilo*	**een pond**	*a pound (500 grams)*
een liter	*a litre*		

In Dutch, you never use a plural for these weights and measures, so *20
kilos* is **20 kilo** and *3 litres* is **3 liter**.

Some examples:

Ik heb 2 kilo appels nodig.	*I need two kilos of apples.*
Ik wil een liter halfvolle melk.	*I want a litre of semi-skimmed milk.*
Ik heb een pot pindakaas, een kuipje boter en een zakje drop nodig.	*I need a jar of peanut butter, a tub of butter and a small bag of liquorice.*

? Test yourself

1 Give three food products and two drinks that you buy most weeks.

2 On which **e** in the word **drieentwintig** should a trema (two dots) be placed?

3 Count out loud from 24 to 39 and then from 39 to 24.

4 Ask: *How much does a bottle of white wine cost?*

5 Say whether the following words are **de** or **het** words:
   a suiker (*sugar*)
   b melk (*milk*)
   c postkantoor (*post office*)
   d brood (*bread*)
   e ding (*thing*)

6 Give the plural form of the following words:
   a de pot (*jar*)
   b de euro
   c de man
   d de foto (*photo*)
   e het meisje (*girl*)

7 When you're in a shop and the shopkeeper asks: **Wie is er aan de beurt?**, would you answer **2 kilo appels** or **Ik**?

8 Give the Dutch for: *I would like a pound of cheese.*

SELF CHECK

I CAN ...
... go shopping.
... ask prices.
... name several kinds of food.

4 Zij houdt van moderne kleren

She likes modern clothes

In this unit you will learn how to:

▶ *talk about your family.*
▶ *talk about likes and dislikes in relation to clothes and food.*
▶ *say that something is yours or someone else's.*

CEFR: (A2) *Can use a series of phrases and sentences to describe family, other people, living conditions, daily routines; can understand sentences and frequently used expressions related to areas of most immediate relevance.*

De familie *The family*

Hallo, dit is mijn familie. Ik ben getrouwd. Mijn man en ik hebben twee kinderen, een zoon en een dochter. Samen vormen we een gezin. Mijn familie is niet groot. Ik heb een vader en moeder (mijn ouders) en een broer en zus. Mijn broer en zus zijn niet getrouwd. Ik heb twee ooms en twee tantes: oom Jan en tante Wil, en oom Arend en Tante Nel. Tante wil is de zus van mijn vader en oom Arend is de broer van mijn moeder. Ik heb nog één oma en één opa, de ouders van mijn moeder.

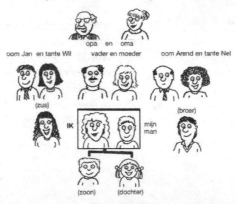

 Hoeveel broers heeft vader, en hoeveel broers heeft moeder?

44

Vocabulary builder 1

Listen to the new words and expressions and fill in the missing English meanings.

de familie	*family*
de moeder	*mother*
de opa	*grandfather*
de oma	*grandmother*
de vader	*father*
de moeder	*mother*
de ouder	*parent*
het kind	*child*
de tante	*aunt*
de oom	*uncle*
de broer	*brother*
de zus	*sister*
de zoon	*son*
de dochter	*daughter*
de man	*husband* (also *man*)
de vrouw	*wife* (also *woman*)
mijn man	*my husband*
mijn vrouw	*my wife*
de vader	_____
het huis	*house*
de tuin	*garden*
de zus	*sister*
slapen	*to sleep*
lezen	*to read*
de krant	*newspaper*
op vakantie	*on holiday*
slapen	*to sleep*
hebben altijd ruzie	*are always arguing*
de plaats	*place*
de kaart	*card*
de sleutel	*key*

The word **gezin** also means *family*, but it refers to a small family unit of parent(s) and children. You will also need to know the following words:

| de jongen | boy |
| het meisje | girl |

Here are the words that you use to indicate that something is yours or someone else's.

mijn	mine
jouw	your (singular informal)
uw	your (singular formal)
zijn	his
haar	_____
ons/onze	our
jullie	your (plural informal)
uw	your (plural formal)
hun	their

New expressions

groot	big
klein	small
lief	sweet, nice
mooi	beautiful, pretty
vervelend	horrible
aardig	nice

In the Netherlands, many children will say **je** and **jij** to their parents, although it is still very common for children to address their parents formally, with **u**. Grandparents are normally addressed with **u**.

Dialogue 1

Tania talks about pictures of her family.

 04.02 Listen to Tania talking about her family and answer the questions.

1 What is her mother doing?

Dit is mijn huis en mijn familie.
Mijn moeder leest de krant.
Mijn vader werkt in de tuin.

2 How many tents does the family have?

Wij zijn hier op vakantie.
Wij hebben twee tenten.
Mijn ouders slapen in hun tent.
Mijn zus en ik slapen in onze tent.

3 Whose brother is Uncle Barend?

Dit zijn oom Barend en tante Miep.
Oom Barend is de broer van mijn moeder.
Oom Barend en tante Miep hebben altijd ruzie.

When speaking informally (and usually quickly), Dutch speakers will abbreviate the forms **mijn** (*my*), **jouw** (*your*) and **zijn** (*his*) to **m'n**, **je** and **z'n**. If you want to stress that something is *mine*, *yours* or *his*, you use the full forms.

Practice 1

1 Look at the family tree at the beginning of this unit as if it showed your own family. You are in the centre. Write sentences about your family using the following words and the verb zijn *to be*. **Make sure you use the correct form of the verb. Make as many sentences as you can. You will find example sentences in the Answer key.**

You will be able to make many sentences. It is therefore important that you check carefully the correct use of the verb and the word **mijn**.

You can use words to describe your relatives. For example:

Mijn opa en oma zijn actief.

Or you could use various professions. Check for these in the previous units. For example:

Mijn oom is politieagent.

You have seen that the word **een** means *one*, but it is also used in Dutch to mean *a/an*. Instead of saying **de tuin** *the garden*, **het huis** *the house*, we can also say **een tuin**, **een huis** (*a garden, a house*). You will see that the word **een** is used for both **de** and **het** words. In the plural, you say **tuinen** (*gardens*), **huizen** (*houses*) and you don't use **een**.

2 Use the family tree and complete the sentences about the relationships within the family. Each sentence should be made up from the point of view of the family member in brackets. For example:

Opa is ... man (oma) → *opa is haar man*

    a oom Jan is ... zoon. (opa)
    b oom Jan is ... broer. (vader)
    c oma is ... moeder. (tante Nel)
    d vader is ... zoon. (oma)
    e moeder is ... vrouw. (vader)
    f tante Nel is ... dochter. (oma)

Vocabulary builder 2

DESCRIPTIVE WORDS

altijd	*always*
vaak	*often*
meestal	*mostly, usually*
nieuw	*new*
dragen	*to wear*
houden van	*to like*
lang	*long*
kort	*short*
sportief	*casual*
strak	*tight*
soms	*sometimes*
het mobieltje	*mobile phone*
het attachékoffertje	*attaché case*
het petje	*cap*
de rugzak	*rucksack*
het kind (plural: kinderen)	*child*het voetbalshirt *football shirt*
chagrijnig	*moody*
erg	*very*
inderdaad	*indeed/that's true*
knap	*handsome*
ik weet het niet	*I don't know*
te laat	*(too) late*
alleen	*only*
Echt?	*Really?*
nogal	*quite*

KLEREN *CLOTHES*

de rok	*skirt*	de laars (plural laarzen)	*boot*
de blouse	*blouse*	de schoen	*shoe*
het overhemd	*shirt*	het pak	*suit*
de broek	*trousers*	het T-shirt	*t-shirt*
de jas	*coat, jacket*	de trui	*sweater*
de spijkerbroek	*jeans*	de jurk	*dress*
de stropdas	*tie*	de panty	*(pair of) tights*
het colbert	*jacket*	de hoed	*hat*
de bril	*glasses*		

KLEUREN *COLOURS*

rood	*red*	geel	*yellow*
blauw	*blue*	groen	*green*
oranje	*orange*	paars	*purple*
bruin	*brown*	grijs	*grey*
wit	*white*	zwart	*black*

Dialogue 2

04.03 Listen to the monologues about Heleen, Henk-Jan and Job and answer the questions.

1 What is Heleen wearing?

Dit is mijn vriendin, Heleen.
Zij draagt altijd nieuwe kleren.
Zij houdt van moderne kleren.
Zij draagt: lange zwarte laarzen,
een korte rode rok en een strakke blouse.

2 What does Henk-Jan wear to work, with his suit?

Dit is mijn vriend Henk-Jan.
Hij draagt vaak een pak voor zijn werk
met een overhemd en een stropdas.
Hij heeft een mobieltje en hij draagt
een attachékoffertje.

3 Does Job wear smart or sporty clothes?

Dit is mijn broer Job.
Hij oefent vaak op zijn skateboard.
Hij draagt meestal sportieve kleren:
een T-shirt en een korte broek.
Soms heeft hij een petje op.
Hij heeft ook vaak een rugzak.

Language discovery

DESCRIPTIVE WORDS

You may have noticed that descriptive words (adjectives) such as **oud**, **nieuw**, **kort**, **strak**, etc. sometimes have an **-e** at the end and sometimes they don't. Look at these sentences:

de jas is <u>oud</u>	**de <u>zwarte</u> broek**
zijn mobieltje is <u>nieuw</u>	**de <u>mooie</u> skateboard**
het blauwe overhemd	*the blue shirt*
een zwarte rugzak	*a black rucksack*
zijn bruine auto	*his brown car*

▶ No **-e** when the descriptive word comes after the thing it describes.
▶ Add **-e** if the description comes before the thing it describes.

There is a snag, though. The **-e** is left out in the following examples:

een dun T-shirt	*a thin T-shirt*
een blauw pak	*a blue suit*

When the descriptive word refers to a **het** word (**het T-shirt**, **het pak**) but is used with **een**, not **het**, you drop the **-e**. But note:

dunne T-shirts, **blauwe pakken**

Naturally when you use several words to describe something or someone, all these words follow the same pattern, for instance:

Mijn kleren zijn oud en vies.

Ik draag oude en vieze kleren. (Note that the spelling of **vies**

changes: see Grammar summary.)

Mijn broer draagt nooit een net, grijs pak.

> **LANGUAGE TIP**
> It is good to remember that there are twice as many **de-** words as **het-** words so descriptive words get an extra **-e** in front of most nouns. Particularly since all plural words are **de-** words.

IK HOU VAN

Josje	Ik hou van moderne kleren, en jij?
Greetje	Ik hou van nette kleren.

Ik hou van is a way of saying what you like. The full verb is **houden van**, so when you talk about someone else you can say, for example: **Zij houdt van klassieke muziek.**

The **ik** form of the verb **houden van** is usually written as **ik hou van** (**ik houd van** is considered too formal).

What do you and the members of your family like?

Ik hou van	**witte wijn.**
Mijn vriend houdt van	**rode paprika** (*peppers*)**.**
Mijn man houdt van	**zwarte kleren.**
Georgia houdt van	**zwemmen** (*swimming*)**.**
Dannie houdt van	**lezen** (*reading*)**.**
Mijn tante houdt van	**fietsen** (*cycling*)**.**

Practice 2

1 **Describe what you and your friend are going to wear tomorrow. Use the following table to help you and start sentences a and b with** ik **and sentence c with** hij**. For example:**

Ik draag mijn witte T-shirt, **mijn blauwe spijkerbroek**, etc.

	wit	blauw	rood	geel
a mijn	T-shirt	spijkerbroek	jas	petje
b een	rok	T-shirt	trui	bril
c een	broek	colbert	overhemd	hoed

2 **Make a list of your own and your relatives' or friends' likes as far as food and drink are concerned. For example:**

Ik hou van bier.

Mijn zus houdt van appels.

3 **Now make a list of your own and your relatives' or friends' likes as far as activities are concerned. For example:**

Ik hou van fietsen.

Mijn vriend John houdt van skateboarden (*skateboarding*)**.**

4 **Complete the sentences and use the information between brackets. You do not have to use de or het. They are given here to help you in using the adjectives correctly. For example:**

Mijn broer Jan houdt van (het bier, koud).

Mijn broer Jan houdt van koud bier.

a Ik hou van (de wijn, wit).

b Jij houdt van (de wijn, rood) hè?

c Jantien ...... (de kleren, zwart).

d Mijn ouders ...... (de huizen, groot).

e Mijn kinderen ...... (de voetbalshirts, oranje).

f Mandy ...... (de kinderen, klein).

5 **04.04 Listen to the people describing their holiday pictures.**

a Which of the following relatives are in the pictures they talk about?
Tick the ones that are mentioned in each case. You can find the full
text of this exercise in the Answer key.

1 vader, moeder, opa, oma, zoon, dochter, zus, broer, oom, tante,
vriend, vriendin

2 vader, moeder, opa, oma, zoon, dochter, zus, broer, oom, tante,
vriend, vriendin

3 vader, moeder, opa, oma, zoon, dochter, zus, broer, oom, tante,
vriend, vriendin

4 vader, moeder, opa, oma, zoon, dochter, zus, broer, oom, tante,
vriend, vriendin

NB **Vriend** means *male friend* and **vriendin** means *female friend*.

b Listen to all the fragments again and indicate what these people
were wearing, if it was mentioned, by filling in the columns.

Persoon	Kleren
1 oma	een grote hoed
2	
3	
4	

Go further

1 **Describe the following pictures and give as much information as
you can about the people in them. Say what they are wearing,
what they like to drink and anything else that you could say
about them. You need to make use of the various words and
patterns you have learnt in this and previous units. For example:**

Jasmijn houdt van wijn.   Jaap houdt van …

Zij draagt …   …

Zij heeft …   …

etc.

2 Describe what you are wearing at the moment. Write the sentences down, then describe what two other people in your environment are wearing. For example:

Ik draag een grijs T-shirt en een korte broek.

Mijn vriendin draagt een strakke blouse en een spijkerbroek.

3 04.05 Listen to the audio of several people talking about others who aren't present. The people who aren't present are given in the following table. Write what is being said about these people in the box next to their name (in English).

Name	What's being said about them
Jolanda	
Willem-Alexander	
Frédérique*	
Jos	

LANGUAGE USE

In the last listening exercise, you will have heard **goh** and **zeg**. Both are used to emphasize what is being said in a statement. **Goh** is used at the beginning of sentences and is often followed by the structure **wat** + description by way of exclamation:

Goh, wat ben jij slim!	*My, you're smart!*
Goh, wat mooi!	*My, that's really beautiful!*

Zeg is only used at the end of sentences in this capacity:

Wat een lekkere soep, zeg!	*This soup is really wonderful!* (more literally: *Such a nice soup!*)
Wat mooi, zeg!	*That's really beautiful!*

> **LANGUAGE TIP**
> There are many small words like **goh**, **zeg** and **wat**. Their meaning can be difficult to decipher, but they make you sound like a real native speaker. One such word is **hoor**, which is used to reassure the person you're speaking to, usually after a yes/no question.

Vind jij dat ook?	*Do you think so too?*
Ja, hoor.	*Yes, sure.*

? Test yourself

1 Answer these questions:
  a Hoeveel broers heb je?
  b Hoeveel zussen heb je?
  c Hoeveel ooms heb je?

2 Say: *This is his mother.*

3 Say: *These are her parents.*

4 Which of the following descriptive words gets an extra **-e**, and which doesn't? Can you explain why?
  a Ik draag een blauw … spijkerbroek.
  b Ik draag een groen ·… overhemd.

5 Say: *I am wearing a white T-shirt.*

6 Describe what you are wearing.

7 Say: *We like red wine.*

8 A friend's young son has made a drawing. Comment on it by saying: *That's really beautiful!*

SELF CHECK

I CAN ...
… talk about your family.
… talk about likes and dislikes in relation to clothes and food.
… say that something is yours or someone else's.

5

Geeft u mij maar een pilsje
A lager for me, please

In this unit you will learn how to:
▶ *order food and drink.*
▶ *discuss what other people would like.*
▶ *discuss relationships.*

CEFR: (A2) *Can find specific, predictable information in simple everyday material such as menus; can explain likes or dislikes.*

Food and drink

Junk food in Holland is provided in abundance in **snackbars** (in Flanders **het frietkot**) selling a whole range of fried food, even vegetarian options. *Chips* or *fries* (in the Netherlands called **patat** and in Belgium **friet**) usually come with a great variety of *sauces* (**sauzen**). The most common one is **mayonaise** and if you ask for **patat met** it is understood you want mayonnaise with your chips. Any other sauce, e.g. **satésaus** (*satay sauce*) needs to be specifically asked for, but there are various set combinations of sauces, some with fanciful names such as **patatje oorlog**, the latter word meaning *war*. A popular choice is **patatje speciaal**, a combination of mayonnaise, tomato ketchup and onions.

In the Netherlands, you can also find some places where you can get your junk food 'out of a wall', frequently at train stations and in large shopping centres. Portions are kept warm in rows of little glass-fronted compartments which open when you insert money.

Tea in the Netherlands and Flanders will always be served without milk. You will need to ask specifically for milk if you want it.

An informal Dutch word for *café*, *bar* or *pub* is **de kroeg**. If people have a favourite pub which they frequent, then this is called their **stamkroeg**, and the person who goes there is **een stamgast**, *a regular*.

What does **met** mean in **patat met**?

Vocabulary builder

een kopje thee		a cup of tea
met melk		with milk
met suiker		with sugar
zonder melk		without milk
zonder suiker		without sugar
een glas sap		a glass of juice
appelsap		apple juice
sinaasappelsap		orange juice
druivensap		grape juice

ananassap	pineapple juice
een glas fris	a cold drink
cassis	sparkling blackcurrant juice
coca cola	Coca-Cola
sinas	sparkling orange
limonade	cordial

de bliklimonade	can of soft drink
jenever	gin
whisky	whisky
de borrel	strong drink

iets bestellen	to order something
Geeft u mij maar …	…, please (lit. Give me …, please)
Mag ik een …?	May I have …?
het pilsje	lager
jus d'orange	orange juice (sometimes the French word is used rather than the Dutch **sinaasappelsap**)
iets	something
eten	to eat

nemen	*to take*
de uitsmijter	*a dish with fried eggs,*
bread	
	and a salad (this is
traditional	
	café fare)
geeft u hun maar …	*give them …*
vruchtensap	*fruit juice*
geitenkaas en tijm	*goat's cheese and thyme*
de schotel	*dish/meal*
Anders nog iets?	*Anything else?*
kroket	*a meat ragout encased in*
	a crispy fried crust
frikadel	*long thin sausage*

New expressions 1

zeggen	*to say* (here: *Can I help you?*)
Ik wil graag een kopje koffie.	*I would like a cup of coffee.*
Een glas rode wijn, graag.	*A glass of red wine, please.*
Iets bestellen	*to order something*
Geeft u mij maar …	*…, please.* (lit. *Give me …, please.*)
Mag ik een …?	*May I have …?*
het pilsje	*lager*
jus d'orange	*orange juice* (sometimes the French word is used rather than the Dutch 'sinaasappelsap')
iets	*something*
eten	*to eat*
nemen	*to take*
de uitsmijter	*a dish with fried eggs, bread and a salad* (this is traditional café fare)
geeft u hun maar …	*give them …*
zitten	*to sit*
Zij hebben dorst.	*They are thirsty.*
te drinken	*to drink*

een lekker drankje	*a nice drink*
voor me	*for me*
jazeker	*certainly*
Zeg het maar?	*What will it be?*
Doe maar een …	*Oh, give me a …*
Zij hebben honger.	*They are hungry.*

Can you ask for a glass of white wine and another of orange juice?

Dialogues

Listen to the following dialogues and answer the questions.

DIALOGUE 1

Merel and Tine are in a café.

05.02 Listen carefully to what they order from the waiter.

1 What does Tine, who orders after Merel, ask for?

Ober	Zegt u het maar.
Merel	Ik wil graag een kopje koffie.
Ober	En u, mevrouw?
Tine	Een glas rode wijn, graag.

2 Now it's your turn to order. This would be how you would order a coffee:

Ik wil graag een kopje koffie.

Een kopje koffie, graag.

- **a** order a glass of orange juice
- **b** order a glass of cordial
- **c** order a strong drink (use the general term)
- **d** ask for a cold drink (use the general term)
- **e** ask for a sparkling blackcurrant drink
- **f** ask for a tea with milk and sugar
- **g** ask for a coffee with milk and without sugar
- **h** ask for a pineapple juice

DIALOGUE 2

In het café. *In the café.*

Listen carefully to what everyone orders.

3   What would the children like to eat?

Ober	Wilt u iets bestellen?
Berend	Geeft u mij maar een pilsje.
Annie	Mag ik een jus d'orange?
Ober	Wilt u ook iets eten?
Annie	Ja, wat neem jij?
Berend	Ik wil graag een uitsmijter.
Annie	Ja voor mij ook.
Ober	Een pilsje, een jus d'orange en twee uitsmijters. En de kinderen?
Annie	Geeft u hun maar patat.

DIALOGUE 3

Chantal has a conversation with a barkeeper.

05.04 Listen carefully to the conversation.

4   Does she ask for a beer?

Barkeeper	Hoi.
Chantal	Hoi. Heb je een lekker drankje voor me?
Barkeeper	Jazeker. Zeg 't maar. Cocktail? Wijntje? Pilsje?
Chantal	Doe maar een wodka.

5 **Compare Dialogues 2 and 3 from this unit and answer the following questions in English.**

  a Which one is more formal, do you think?
  b Can you think of a few ways in which the language makes one dialogue more formal than the other?

6 **This is a description of Tine and Merel (see the first dialogue in this unit):**

Tine en Merel zitten in een restaurant. Zij hebben dorst. Zij bestellen iets te drinken. Merel wil een kopje koffie en Tine neemt een glas rode wijn.

Write a similar account of the story of Berend, Annie and the children in a restaurant and Chantal in the café. Use the verbs nemen, willen and bestellen, **but not the verb** geven**. There will thus be several possible variations, but in the key you will find an example. Think about the correct form of the verb.**

You might want to give your sentences a little more meaning by adding some other verbs, e.g. houden van. **You might also want to make your sentences sound more authentic by adding words such as** maar **to show contrast, or** ook **to show similarities. For example:** Merel wil koffie, maar Tine neemt wijn. *Merel wants coffee, but Tine is having wine.*

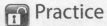 Practice

1 Order each of the following, using a variety of expressions. For example:

Geeft u mij maar een jus d'orange.

Mag ik een jus d'orange?

Doe maar een jus d'orange.

Een jus d'orange, graag.

    a a glass of white wine

    b a cup of tea stuk

    c an uitsmijter

    d a gin

    e a grape juice

    f a piece of apple pie (**het** means *the piece*)

    g a salad

    h a pizza

2 Mark whether the following food orders are formal or informal.

    a Een fles witte wijn graag.

    b Ik wil een spa rood, alstublieft.

    c Doe maar vruchtensap.

    d Een bruin bolletje met geitenkaas en tijm, graag.

    e Geeft u mij maar de aspergesoep.

    f Voor mij een tonijnsalade, alstublieft.

    g Ik wil graag de vegetarische schotel, alstublieft.

ALSTUBLIEFT, ALSJEBLIEFT *YOU'RE WELCOME*

These words literally mean *if you please*, and are frequently used in ordering, where it has the same meaning as the word **graag**, which you have already encountered. In the Netherlands and in Belgium people also say **alstublieft/alsjeblieft** when giving something. This is a very common practice, whether you are giving a present, are passing round papers in a business meeting, or are handing over money at the checkout in the supermarket. **Alstublieft** is more polite than **alsjeblieft** because it uses the pronoun **u**. You use it in situations where you would address someone with **u** rather than **je/jij**.

64

Language discovery

You have now learnt to perform several functions in Dutch. You can use various phrases for ordering in a restaurant, you can shop, you can introduce yourself and ask for specific information from others and you can say something about yourself and your family.

In addition you have started to manipulate the language itself. You can form simple sentences and you have learnt to talk about things which are yours or other people's (possessives) and you have learnt to add extra information to words to describe them (adjectives).

In this unit you have been introduced to a new pattern:

Geeft u mij maar een pilsje.

Geeft u hun maar patat.

There are actually two new patterns within these sentences.

▶ The first is that there is a change in word order: **geeft u mij ...** instead of **u geeft**. This sentence is not a statement as such, but in fact gives a command of what you should give to me. However, this phrase in combination with the word **maar** performs the function of ordering in a restaurant. You will learn more about this pattern in Unit 10.

▶ The second new pattern you have learnt in this unit is where you are introduced to new words to refer to people. As you know, the words **ik**, **jij**, **hij**, etc. are used to refer to the people the sentence is about, the **subjects**. People or things who don't actually do something in the sentence are called **objects**. As in English we use different words (object pronouns) to refer to them: **mij**, **jou**, **hem**, etc. (*me, you, him*).

So we may have:

Zij kust hem.   *She kisses him.*

She is doing the action (**kust**) and he is at the receiving end of it. So he is the object and therefore we refer to him as **hem**.

Here is a list of these object pronouns:

mij	*me*	**ons**	*us*
jou	*you*	**jullie**	*you*
u	*you*	**u**	*you*
hem	*him*	**hen/hun/ze**	*them*
haar	*her*		

Frequently, these words are combined with prepositions (words such as *to*, *from*, *with*, *on*, etc.). For example:

Ik werk samen met hem aan een project.   *I work together with him on a project.*

Complete the sentences and substitute the words in brackets with an object pronoun:

  a Herman werkt met _____ (Tania).
  b Geef _____ (ik) maar een stukje appeltaart.
  c Jaap helpt _____ (Jan en Luuk).
  d Kees woont met _____ (wij) samen (samen = *together*).
  e Is dit van _____ (jij)?
  f Ik kus _____ (mijn man).

New expressions 2

verliefd zijn op	*to be in love with, to fancy*
niet	*not*
volgens …	*according to …*
Echt?	*Really?*
gek zijn op	*to fancy*
gaan met …	*to go out with …*
zag	*saw*
zoenen	*to kiss*

05.05 Listen to the following conversation between two girls on a bus.

Claire is verliefd op Jack.
Echt? Maar hij is niet verliefd op … Hij is volgens … (me) gek op Anita.
Maar Anita gaat toch met Bart?
Nee hoor. Bart is gek op Maarten. En Maarten ook op …
Echt?
Ja, ik zag … samen zoenen.

Test yourself

1 A waiter in a café says **Zegt u het maar**. Order two cups of coffee, a cola and an orange juice.

2 Order the following things. Try to do it in different ways:
   a pizza
   b fries with mayonnaise
   c coffee with milk and without sugar

3 Say: *I am hungry.*

4 Say: *They are thirsty.*

5 Say: *Juliet kisses Jake.*

6 Fill in the correct form of the verb**: Ty (werken) samen met een collega aan een nieuw product.** (*Ty is working with a colleague on a new product.*)

7 Fill in the correct form of the verb: **(Werken) jij samen met Ty?**

8 Fill in the missing word: **Gabriella is verliefd ... Peter-Jan.**

9 Replace Gabriella and Peter-Jan in the previous question with one of the following words: **ik**, **mij**, **zij**, **hij**, **wij**, **hem**, **haar**, **jou**, **jij**.

10 Tell a friend: *Robert is in love with you.*

I CAN ...
○ ... order food and drink.
○ ... discuss what other people would like.
○ ... discuss relationships.

6

Ga je vaak naar de bioscoop?

Do you go to the cinema a lot?

In this unit you will learn how to:
▶ *ask yes and no questions.*
▶ *answer yes and no questions.*
▶ *say what country you are from.*
▶ *fill in a form.*

CEFR: (A2) *Can cope with a limited number of follow-up questions if some repetition is possible.*

 ## De camping *Camping*

Going camping, **kamperen**, is very popular in the Low Countries. Lots of families spend their holidays at home or abroad on **een camping** *a campsite*. People stay in **een tent** or **een caravan**, but at some campsites you can also rent **huisjes** *cottages* or **trekkershutten** *cabins*. These have less in the way of luxury but are still very popular, particularly with people on cycling holidays – very popular in the Low Countries – and have the advantage of being cheaper. Campsites are, on the whole, geared more towards individual choice and offer fewer organized activities than in some other countries.

What would you stay in on a campsite?

V Vocabulary builder

Listen to the new words and expressions.

of	*or*
allebei	*both*
daar	*there*
al lang	*for a long time*
sinds	*since*
vorig jaar	*last year*
bouwkunde	*architecture*
voor	*for*
de persoon	*person*
de douche	*shower*
Hoelang?	*How long?*
de nacht	*night*
duur	*expensive*

New expressions

Waar komt u vandaan?	*Where do you come from?*
het adres	*address*
het telefoonnummer	*phone number*
camping	*campsite/ground*
het huisje	*cabin, cottage*
de trekkershut	*cabin/hiker's hut*
mobiel	*mobile*
kopen	*to buy*
vroeg	*early*
het programma	*programme*

Language discovery 1

LANDEN EN NATIONALITEITEN *COUNTRIES AND NATIONALITIES*

Sometimes when referring to your nationality you use different words, depending on whether you are male or female, for example, **ik ben Engelsman** *I am English* (male) or **ik ben Engelse** *I am English* (female). However, people often use the words given in the following list, for instance, **ik ben Engels** *I am English*. When in front of an object, idea or person, you may need to add an **-e**. Look at these examples:

Belgische chocola   **Franse kaas**

Nederlandse tulpen   **Brits rundvlees**

06.02

Nederland	*the Netherlands*	Nederlands	*Dutch*
België	*Belgium*	**Belgisch**	*Belgian*
Vlaanderen	*Flanders*	**Vlaams**	*Flemish*
Engeland	*England*	**Engels**	*English*
Groot-Brittannië	*Great Britain*	**Brits**	*British*
Schotland	*Scotland*	**Schots**	*Scottish*
Frankrijk	*France*	**Frans**	*French*
Duitsland	*Germany*	**Duits**	*German*
Italië	*Italy*	**Italiaans**	*Italian*
Spanje	*Spain*	**Spaans**	*Spanish*
Amerika	*America*	**Amerikaans**	*American*
Ierland	*Ireland*	**Iers**	*Irish*
China	*China*	**Chinees**	*Chinese*
Europa	*Europe*	**Europees**	*European*

1 **06.03** You're at a Dutch course in the Netherlands. All students
   are asked what nationality they are. Give their answers.
   For example:

meneer Callenbach *(Dutch)* → *Ik ben Nederlands.*

   a Jean Roach (American)
   b Françoise Le Lerre (French)
   c Tony Jackson (Irish)
   d mevrouw Wong (Chinese)
   e Mary Brander (Scottish)
   f Annette Braun (German)

2 **Uit welk land?** *From where?* **Fill in the gap, using the word in
   brackets as a guide). For example:**

Ik hou van _____ humor (Engeland). → *Ik hou van Engelse
humor.* (*I like English humour.*)

   a Jack houdt van _____ kaas (Nederland).
   b Cynthia koopt meestal _____ chips (Amerika).
   c Ik hou van _____ whisky (Schotland).
   d Ik eet vaak _____ brood (Duitsland). (NB het brood)
   e Mijn man draagt vaak _____ kleren (Italië).
   f Wij drinken meestal _____ wijn (Spanje).
   g Tony luistert vaak naar _____ muziek (Ierland).
   h Chris kijkt meestal naar _____ tv-programma's (Groot-Brittannië).

Dialogue

Dennis is at the campsite reception desk.

06.04 Listen to the conversation and answer the questions.

1 For how long does Dennis want the house?

Dennis	Ik wil graag een huisje voor twee personen.
Receptioniste	Voor hoelang?
Dennis	Voor twee nachten.
Receptioniste	Ik heb een trekkershut, met toilet, maar zonder douche.
Dennis	Dat is goed. Hoe duur is het?
Receptioniste	30 euro nacht.
Dennis	Prima.
Receptioniste	Wat is uw naam?
Dennis	Dennis Johnson.
Receptioniste	Waar komt u vandaan?
Dennis	Ik ben Engels. Ik kom uit Engeland.
Receptioniste	U spreekt goed Nederlands.
Dennis	Dank u.
Receptioniste	Heeft u een adres in Nederland?
Dennis	Ja. Burgweg 35, Papendrecht.
Receptioniste	En een telefoonnummer?
Dennis	Ik heb een mobiel nummer: 00 44 7953 774326.

2 Hoe duur is het huisje?

3 Waar komt Dennis vandaan?

4 Wat is het adres van Dennis in Nederland?

5 Wat is het telefoonnummer van Dennis?

Language discovery 2

YES/NO QUESTIONS

06.05

During a job interview

Meneer Vriesekoop	Woont u hier in de buurt?
Francesca	Ja, ik woon hier in de buurt.

Between friends

Anna	Kom je morgen?
Dienke	Nee, ik kom morgen niet.

Leaving a restaurant

Ober	Is dit uw jas?
Mevrouw Boon	Nee, dat is mijn jas niet.

At home

Edith	Heb jij de autosleutels? (*car keys*)
Arend	Nee, ik heb de autosleutels niet.

Let us look first at the questions. You will notice that the word order changes when you ask a yes/no question. As in questions with a question word, the verb now comes before the person or thing that the sentence is about. Look carefully at the sentences **Kom je morgen?** and **Heb jij de autosleutels?** Remember that when you ask a question using **jij**, you need to drop the **-t** (unless it is part of the verb, e.g. **eten**: **jij eet → eet jij?**).

Answering a yes/no question with a *yes* is straightforward. You just make a simple statement and do not have to change the word order. When you want to respond to a question in the negative, you need to add **niet** (*not*) to the sentence.

In the earlier examples, **niet** came at the end of the sentence. This is often the case, although **niet** is a tricky word and there are various places that **niet** can go in the sentence depending on the sentence structure.

Look at these examples:

Regina	Woon jij ook in Amsterdam?
Harry	Nee, ik woon niet in Amsterdam.
Ineke	Werk jij in Leeuwarden?
Frieda	Nee, ik werk niet in Leeuwarden.
Larry	Hou je van tomaten?
Hans	Nee, ik hou niet van tomaten.
Hanna	Ben je hier op vakantie?
Anke	Nee, ik ben hier niet op vakantie.

In these examples **niet** comes before words which tell us about the way or direction something is done, where it is, etc. These words, such as **met**, **in** and **op**, are called prepositions.

Now look at these examples:

Ans	Zijn jouw schoenen nieuw?
Katy	Nee, mijn schoenen zijn niet nieuw.
Desiree	Werkt de radio goed? (Is the radio working well?)
Lex	Nee, de radio werkt niet goed.

Niet also comes before descriptive words like **nieuw** and **goed** (or adjectives and adverbs, to get a little technical).

You're going on holiday with a friend. There's a lot that still needs to be organized. Your friend is checking to see what you are doing, but because you are busy with work, you can't really do anything. Give negative answers and tell him/her that you're too busy (Ik heb het te druk). **For example:**

Bel jij het hotel? *Nee, ik bel het hotel niet. Ik heb het te druk.*

- **a** Boek jij de tickets?
- **b** Bestel jij de taxi? (**bestellen** *to order*)
- **c** Organiseer jij de excursies? (*to organize the excursions*)
- **d** Pak jij de koffers? (*to pack the suitcases*)
- **e** Koop jij de malariapillen? (*malaria pills/tablets*)
- **f** Wissel jij het geld? (*to change the money*)

Practice 1

06.06 Answer the following questions from your own perspective. Answer with a whole sentence. In the key you will find both the positive and negative answer.

- **a** Hou je van moderne kleren?
- **b** Houdt u van grote tuinen?
- **c** Werk je in Groningen?
- **d** Woont u in Amersfoort?
- **e** Zijn je schoenen oud?
- **f** Drink je graag thee zonder melk? (NB **graag** is an adverb here)
- **g** Bent u de nieuwe manager?
- **h** Zijn de bananen duur? (NB **duur** is an adjective here)
- **i** Gaat u naar uw werk?
- **j** Is dit je jas?

Language discovery 3

Look at the following dialogues:

Richard	Lees je een boek?
Karin	Nee ik lees geen boek.

Nico	Eet je kaas?
Lena	Nee, ik eet geen kaas.

Marianne	Heb je appels?
Ine	Nee, ik heb geen appels.

Geen means *no/not any*. In Dutch, you don't say *I do not have a book*, you say *I have no book*. But:

Ik heb een boek	→	Ik heb geen boek
Ik heb het boek	→	Ik heb het boek niet
Ik heb mijn boek	→	Ik heb mijn boek niet

Geen is used when you say you have no book at all. **Niet** is used to say you don't have a particular book.

1 06.07 Practise answering with geen **by completing the following mini-dialogues. Do this exercise while you listen. Answer all these questions in the negative:**

a Drink je melk?
b Koop je appels?
c Eet je chocola?
d Spreek je Frans?
e Heb je kinderen?
f Neem je een uitsmijter?
g Wil je een slaatje?
h Breng jij een pizza?

2 **06.08** Unfortunately, things are not going as planned and you're having to give negative answers to all the following questions.

  a Hebt u een auto?
  b Woont u in de buurt?
  c Hebt u ervaring? (*experience*)
  d Hebt u diploma's?
  e Werkt u graag?
  f Bent u punctueel? (*punctual*)

3 Now practise checking information you have about people on a list by asking yes/no questions. Formulate your questions according to patterns you know. For example:

Bent u meneer Plantinga?

Woon jij in Heerenveen?

Is jouw adres Turfstraat 24?

  a Meneer Plantinga
     woonplaats: Harderwijk
     beroep: politieagent
     adres: Pijlslaan 15
     postcode: 2586 AL
     telefoonnummer: 4326781

  b Kaatje Lijbers
     woonplaats: Heerenveen
     beroep: verpleegster
     adres: Seringenlaan 18
     postcode: 1864 KN
     telefoonnummer: 567392

Practice 2

1 **06.09** Read and listen to the conversation. Kim has just met Remi in a bar and now they are exchanging more information about themselves.

Kim	Werk je of studeer je?
Remi	Allebei. Ik studeer bouwkunde, maar in het weekend werk ik in een restaurant.
Kim	Werk je daar al lang?
Remi	Sinds vorig jaar.

> **LANGUAGE TIP**
> As in English you can connect short sentences by using words like **en** (*and*), **maar** (*but*) and **of** (*or*).

2 Continue the dialogue. As Remi gives his last answer he asks Kim for information about himself. He also wants to know whether Kim works or studies. Can you think of a way that Remi can change the topic of conversation from himself to Kim? Use the following information to develop your dialogue. Kim says he works. He is a teacher at a school in Amsterdam and has worked there for two years. (Note that the preposition to use for *at a school* **is** op).

3 Looking at the following example, answer the first three questions (a, b, c) from the previous exercise in the negative:

naar de bioscoop (*the cinema*) gaan

Ga je naar de bioscoop?

Nee, ik ga niet naar de bioscoop.

   a naar de radio luisteren
   b naar restaurants gaan
   c naar feesten gaan

And now answer the last four (d, e, f, g) following this example:

Leest u boeken?

Nee, ik lees geen boeken.

   d wijn drinken
   e Frans spreken
   f pizza's eten
   g spijkerbroeken dragen

4 **06.10 Listen to the audio and fill in the form.**

Naam

Beroep

Nationaliteit

Woonplaats

Postcode

Telefoonnummer

5 Now fill in the form with your own details.

Naam

Beroep

Nationaliteit

Woonplaats

Postcode

Telefoonnummer

LANGUAGE TIP

Sometimes you will not only be asked for your telephone number, but also for your mobile or cell phone number: **het mobiele nummer**. A *mobile phone* is usually called **de mobiel** or **het mobieltje**. Since all mobile phone numbers in the Netherlands start with 06, people also use the term **het 06-nummer**.

Test yourself

1 Make the following sentences negative using **niet**:
   a Johanna komt uit België.
   b We houden van strandvakanties.
   c Hij is de nieuwe directeur.

2 Give a negative answer using **geen**:
   a Heb je een auto?
   b Wil Saskia een biertje?
   c Spreken jullie Duits?

3 Give a negative answer using **niet** or **geen**:
   a Heb je ervaring?
   b Werken Joost en zijn vriend hard?
   c Woon jij in Groningen?
   d Neem jij een patatje met?

4 Finish the sentences, following this example: **Klaas komt uit Frankrijk, hij is Frans**.
   a Meike komt uit Duitsland, zij is _____
   b Isa komt uit Nederland, zij is _____
   c Mary en Li komen uit Amerika, zij zijn _____

I CAN ...
... ask yes and no questions.
... answer yes and no questions.
... say what country I am from.
... fill in a form.Naam

7 Wat ga je doen?
What are you going to do?

In this unit you will learn:
▶ *how to talk about your interests.*
▶ *how to talk about the week ahead.*
▶ *how to say what you have to do.*
▶ *how to say what you want to do.*
▶ *how to say what you are going to do.*

CEFR: (A2) *Can discuss what to do next, make and respond to suggestions.*

Museumplein

Amsterdam houses many well-known museums. Some of the most famous ones are grouped around **Het Museumplein** or *Museum Square*. These museums are **Het Rijksmuseum**, the Netherlands' national collection of art and historical artefacts, **Het Van Gogh Museum**, housing the world's most extensive collection of works by Dutch artist Vincent van Gogh, and **Het Stedelijk Museum**, a museum for modern and contemporary art. In addition, **Het Concertgebouw**, a renowned concert hall for (mainly) classical music, is situated on **Museumplein** as well. Note that the residential area south of the concert hall is called **De Concertgebouwbuurt**, *the Concertgebouw quarter*.

Of course there are many more museums in Amsterdam, let alone the rest of The Netherlands. These range from smaller museums like Amsterdam's **Museum Ons' Lieve Heer op Solder** (*Our Dear Lord in the Attic*), a 17th century town house with a hidden catholic church in the attic, and **Het Kröller-Müller Museum**, which displays its 19th and 20th centry art in **Het Nationale Park De Hoge Veluwe** (*Hoge Veluwe National Park*), to **Het Mauritshuis** in the Hague, which houses the country's royal collection of art from the Dutch Golden Age.

Do you know any other museums in The Netherlands? And how about museums in Belgium? What is exhibited in these museums?

V Vocabulary builder

morgen	*tomorrow*
het voetbal	*football (the sport)*
moeten	*to have to (must)*
spelen	*to play*
tegen	*against*
interessant	*interesting*
zwemmen	*to swim*
sporten	*to play sport*
schaatsen	*to skate*
een e-mail aan je vriend sturen	*to send an email to your friend*
de school opbellen	*to phone the school*
in een restaurant eten	*to eat in a restaurant*
boodschappen doen	*to do shopping*
dansen	*to dance*
je huis schilderen	*to paint your house*
je vriend e-mailen	*to email your friend*
schoonmaken	*to clean*
pianospelen	*to play the piano*
zullen	*shall*
de tentoonstelling	*exhibition*
Ik kan … niet	*I can't …*
afspreken	*to make an appointment*
Hoe laat zullen we afspreken	*What time shall we say?*
de ingang	*entrance*
Tot morgen.	*See you tomorrow.*
dan	*then*

> **LANGUAGE TIP**
> Instead of *jouw vriend* or *jouw huis* you can use *je vriend* or *je huis*. *Je* is unstressed. With *jouw* you stress the fact that it's *your* friend and *your* house, and not someone else's.

New expressions

vanochtend	*this morning*
vanmiddag	*this afternoon*
vanavond	*this evening*
morgen	*tomorrow*
overmorgen	*the day after tomorrow*
volgende	*week next week*
volgende maand	*next month*
volgend jaar	*next year*
dagen van de week	*days of the week*
maandag	*Monday*
dinsdag	*Tuesday*
woensdag	*Wednesday*
donderdag	*Thursday*
vrijdag	*Friday*
zaterdag	*Saturday*
zondag	*Sunday*
de ochtend/de morgen	*morning*
de middag	*afternoon*
de avond	*evening*
het huiswerk	*homework*
het artikel	*(reading) article*
Maria's verjaardag vieren	*celebrate Maria's birthday*
langs de dijk fietsen	*cycle along the dyke*
mijn haar wassen	*to wash my hair*
in de tuin werken	*to work in the garden*
les 6 herhalen	*to revise lesson 6*
eten koken	*to cook dinner (literally: to cook food)*
mijn zoon met zijn huiswerk helpen	*to help my son with his homework*

naar het feest van Maria gaan	*to go to Maria's party*
een cadeau voor Maria kopen	*to buy a present for Maria*
foto's in het museum maken	*to take pictures in the museum*
mam/pap bezoeken	*visit mum/dad*

Dialogue 1

Anke asks her friend Richard about the football match tomorrow.

1 07.02 Listen to the conversation. Is Richard interested in football?

Anke	Ga je morgen naar het voetbal kijken?
Richard	Nee, ik moet morgen werken.
Anke	Maar Ajax speelt tegen Manchester United!
Richard	Ik vind voetbal niet interessant.

2 You're talking to your friend, Marijke. She asks you what you are going to do tomorrow. Answer her by using the activities provided.

Wat ga je morgen doen? (dancing) → *Ik ga morgen dansen.*

- **a** phone the school
- **b** skating
- **c** swimming
- **d** eat in a restaurant

3 Now ask Marijke what she has to do tomorrow and give her answers. Use moeten. For example:

to work

Moet je morgen werken?

Ja, ik moet morgen werken.

- **a** to do the shopping
- **b** to paint her house
- **c** to email her friend
- **d** to clean

Dialogue 2

Ellie and Heleen are having a conversation.

1 07.03 **Now listen to these two conversations. Is Heleen going swimming tomorrow?**

Ellie	Ga je morgen schaatsen?
Heleen	Nee, ik ga morgen niet schaatsen.
Ellie	Ga je morgen zwemmen?
Heleen	Nee, ik ga morgen niet zwemmen.

As you have seen, the position of **niet** in the sentence varies. Notice where it comes in these two examples. However, note also the following examples:

Ellie	Ga je morgen in een restaurant eten?
Heleen	Nee, ik ga morgen niet in een restaurant eten.
Ellie	Ga je morgen boodschappen doen?
Heleen	Nee, ik ga morgen geen boodschappen doen.

2 **Now make up your own mini-dialogue by asking your friend, Marijke, whether she is going to do the following activities tomorrow. Answer for her, saying that she is not, and give an alternative activity, using the niet pattern. For example, ask Marijke whether she is going to dance tomorrow:**

You	*Ga je morgen dansen?*
Marijke	*Nee, ik ga morgen niet dansen, maar ik ga mijn vriend e-mailen.*

  a Ask whether she is going to phone the school tomorrow.
  b Ask whether she is going to skate tomorrow.
  c Ask whether she is going to swim tomorrow.
  d Ask whether she is going to cycle tomorrow (**fietsen**).
  e Ask her whether she is going to eat in a restaurant tomorrow.

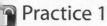 Practice 1

1 Look at Jeroen's diary. For each day, say what he's going to/has to do. For example:

Maandag gaat hij zwemmen.

MAANDAG zwemmen	DONDERDAG Janine bellen	
DINSDAG boodschappen doen	VRIJDAG dansen	
WOENSDAG schoonmaken	ZATERDAG voetballen	ZONDAG Mam/pap bezoeken

2 07.04 **Ask Frans whether he is going to eat in a Chinese restaurant this evening. For example:**

Ga je vanavond in een Chinees restaurant eten?

  a Ask Frans whether he is going to go dancing the day after tomorrow.
  b Ask him if he is going to play sports (**sporten**) this evening.
  c Ask him if he is going to work next week.
  d Ask him if he is going to go shopping this afternoon.
  e Ask him if he is going to paint his house next year.

> **LANGUAGE TIP**
> If you are lucky enough to know a native speaker who is prepared to help you with vocabulary, you could ask him or her to help you to extend the list of activities to fit in with your own situation. You can then write out an activity plan for yourself, whether based on work or on leisure interests, using the following pattern:
> **Ik ga vanavond televisie kijken.**
> **Ik ga volgend jaar een nieuwe baan zoeken.** (*look for a new job*)

Language discovery 1

In this unit you have been using a new word pattern. Can you detect what was different?

The difference is that you have been using two verbs in the same sentence. The first one, the main verb, is where you expect it to be, either at the start of the sentence in a question or as the second item in other sentences. The form of this verb changes depending on who or what the sentence is about. For example, if the question **Ga je morgen naar het voetbal kijken?** were changed into whether Frans were going to watch football, it would be: **Gaat Frans morgen naar het voetbal kijken?**

The second verb in these sentences comes right at the end. This verb at the end does not change its form and is called the infinitive. There doesn't always have to be a second verb in the sentence. For instance, you could have asked:

Ga je morgen naar het Stedelijk? (*musem of modern/contemporary art in Amsterdam*)

de universiteit? (*the university*)

de kroeg? (*bar/café*)

de bioscoop? (*the cinema*)

de schouwburg? (*the theatre*)

het concert? de stad? (*town, to go shopping* or *to go out*)

je werk? (*work*, literally: *your work*)

No second verb is needed here.

Practise these questions.

In our first dialogue, Richard replied that he wasn't interested in football. He could have said:

Ik hou niet van voetbal.

You can also use the phrase **ik ben (niet) geïnteresseerd in ...**:

Ik ben niet geïnteresseerd in voetbal.   *I'm not interested in football.*

Practice 2

1 07.05 **Say that you are not interested in the following:**
   a moderne kunst (*modern art*)
   b politiek (*politics*)
   c sciencefiction
   d sport
   e popmuziek (*pop music*)

2 07.06 **Say that you are interested in the following:**
   a klassieke muziek (*classical music*)
   b Nederlandse literatuur (*Dutch literature*)
   c autotechniek (*car engineering*)
   d toneel (*drama*)

3 **Now look at all the various interests in the previous exercise and give a more nuanced view of what you think of them by including the following phrases:**

ik ben vreselijk geïnteresseerd in …	*I'm terribly/very interested in …*
vooral	*I'm especially interested in …*
nogal	*I'm quite interested in …*
minder	*I'm less interested in …*
niet echt	*I'm not really interested in …*
helemaal niet	*I'm not at all interested in …*

> **LANGUAGE TIP**
> **Heel** and **erg** (*very*) can both be used to say something is *very* … For instance: **heel interessant** (*very interesting*), **erg mooi** (*very beautiful*). They can also be used together to make an even stronger impression: **heel erg lelijk** (*incredibly ugly*). Note that **heel** always comes before **erg**.

4 **Fill in the gaps.**
   a Welke dag is het vandaag? Vandaag is het _____.
   b Welke dag is het morgen? Morgen is het _____.
   c De dagen in het weekend zijn _____.
   d De dag na woensdag is _____. (**na** means *after*)
   e De dag voor woensdag is _____. (**voor** means *before*)
   f De dag na zondag is _____.
   g De dag voor zaterdag is _____.

Dialogue 3

Annemieke and Josje are having a conversation.

 07.07 Listen to the conversation and answer the questions.

1 Is Annemieke able to go to see the new exhibition at the Stedelijk the next day?

Annemieke	Wat zullen we morgen doen?
Josje	Zullen we naar de nieuwe tentoonstelling in het Stedelijk gaan?
Annemieke	Ja leuk. O nee, ik kan morgen niet.
Josje	Vrijdag dan?
Annemieke	Ja, vrijdag is oké.
Josje	Hoe laat zullen we afspreken?
Annemieke	Om half elf bij de ingang?
Josje	Goed. Tot morgen dan.

2 Create your own conversation, based on the dialogue above, using the following information: Ask what you and your partner should do on Saturday. Your partner suggests going to a Chinese restaurant. You are keen, but you can't make it on Saturday, but you can on Sunday. Arrange to meet at 2.15 at the entrance.

Language discovery 2

MODAL VERBS 1

You may have noticed that the pattern of two verbs in a sentence is fairly common. However, you can combine only a few verbs with an infinitive (the full verb at the end). The most common ones are the modal verbs: **zullen** (*shall*), **mogen** (*may*), **moeten** (*must*), **kunnen** (*can*) and **willen** (*want*). These verbs are irregular, so you have to learn the various forms.

zullen	mogen	moeten	kunnen	willen
ik zal	ik mag	ik moet	ik kan	ik wil
jij zal	jij mag	jij moet	jij kan	jij wil
u zal	u mag	u moet	u kan	u wil
hij/zij zal	hij/zij mag	hij/zij moet	hij/zij kan	hij/zij wil
het zal	het mag	het moet	het kan	het wil
wij zullen	wij mogen	wij moeten	wij kunnen	wij willen
jullie zullen	jullie mogen	jullie moeten	jullie kunnen	jullie willen
u zal	u mag	u moet	u kan	u wilt
zij zullen	zij mogen	zij moeten	zij kunnen	zij willen

TIME EXPRESSIONS

7 maandagavond: met Tine naar de bioscoop gaan

8 dinsdagmorgen: een appeltaart maken

9 woensdagochtend: mijn huiswerk maken

10 donderdag

11 vridagmiddag: het artikel over moderne kunst lezen

12 zaterdag

13 zondag

The words for *morning, afternoon* and *evening* are placed after the names of the weekdays to indicate specifically which part of the day you are talking about. For example:

donderdagmiddag

vrijdagavond

dinsdagochtend or dinsdagmorgen

> **LANGUAGE TIP**
> There is no difference between **ochtend** or **morgen**. Both mean *morning*.
> **Wat ga je donderdagmiddag doen?**
> **Donderdagmiddag ga ik mevrouw Kooistra met haar taallessen helpen.**
> Or:
> **Ik ga donderdagmiddag mevrouw Kooistra met haar taallessen helpen.**
> *(Thursday afternoon I am going to help Mrs Kooistra with her language lessons.)*

Note that when you make a statement, you can begin the sentence with a word other than the subject. Often expressions of time, e.g. **morgen** or **zaterdag**, occupy this place in the sentence. However, when this happens, the verb remains in second position and then the subject comes straight after the verb. In a question, however, where the sentence begins either with a question word or with the verb, you cannot put expressions of time in front of them.

Practice 3

JAN'S DIARY

1 Ask Jan what he is going to do on the days listed in his diary and also provide his response. Say it out loud first and then write it down. Make sure you alter the form of the main verb as necessary.

2 Marjan is asking you about Jan's activities. She wants to know what he is going to do on Saturday afternoon and Sunday morning. Make a mini-dialogue with her questions and your answers.

KEES AND MARIA'S DIARY

3 **Ask Kees and Maria what they are going to do on these days and provide the answers.**

4 **Piet is asking you what Kees and Maria are doing on Friday evening and Saturday morning. Make a mini-dialogue with his questions and your answers.**

5 **Use the verbs** gaan, mogen, moeten, willen **and** kunnen **to make sentences about these activities listed. Which verb you use depends on what seems appropriate to you, whether you** can, want, are allowed **or** have to do **these activities. In the Answer key you will find some sample sentences. You can then write several sentences about what you** want to, can, may **or** must do. **For example:**

Ik moet mijn haar wassen.

Ik wil in de tuin werken.

Language discovery 3

MODAL VERBS 2

You have now learnt to say that you can, must, want to or are going to do something. Look at the following sentences to see how you say you do not want to, can't or mustn't do something:

Ik kan morgen geen cadeau voor Maria kopen.

Je mag hier geen foto's maken.

We said in Unit 6 that **niet** normally comes at the end of a sentence:

Ik kom morgen niet.

We also saw that **niet** is placed before prepositions and descriptive words:

Wij gaan niet naar het concert.

Mijn auto is niet nieuw.

Now look at the following sentences with two verbs and have a look at the position of **niet**:

Ik kan mijn zoon niet helpen.

Ik wil les zes niet herhalen.

> **LANGUAGE TIP**
> As you can see, if there's a verb at the end of the sentence (like **helpen** and **herhalen** in these sentences), **niet** is placed in front of it.

🔓 Test yourself

1 Say: *I am going to go cycling tomorrow.*

2 Say: *We have to work tomorrow.*

3 Say: *Henk is not going to do the shopping on Tuesday.*

4 Ask Carla whether she is going to watch television tonight.

5 Say how much you are interested (or not) in the following things:
   a football – not really
   b films – quite
   c politiek – especially

6 Make suggestions to your friends, saying you can do the following things. Add the day on which you could undertake these things:
   a in een restaurant eten – Wednesday
   b go to the cinema – Friday
   c play sports – Sunday

7 Say you can't join your friends on a particular day, because of the following reasons:

8 Example: Sunday – zwemmen. Answer: *Ik kan niet, ik moet zondag zwemmen.*
   a Monday – wash my hair
   b Thursday – do the shopping
   c Tuesday – work

SELF CHECK

I CAN ...	
○	... talk about interests.
○	... talk about the week ahead.
○	... say what I have to do.
○	... say what I want to do.
○	... say what I are going to do.

8

Dat is stukken duurder
That's much more expensive

In this unit you will learn how to:
▶ *compare things.*

CEFR: (A2) *Can use simple descriptive language to make brief statements about and compare objects and possession.*

 Skating

Skeeleren is *in-line skating*. This is very popular in the Netherlands. There are **skeeler** races, clubs, organized tours and you can buy **skeeler** maps and books describing suggested routes. This popularity can probably be explained by the association with ice-skating.

Whenever the ice in the canals is thick enough, ice-skating tours are organized, the most famous of which is **de elfstedentocht**. This momentous 200-kilometre tour past eleven towns in Friesland in the north is something which generates great feelings of national pride and festivity.

Can you say, in Dutch, how long **de elfstedentocht** tour is?

Vocabulary builder

08.01 Listen to the new words and expressions.

vragen	*to ask*
de bloem	*flower*
rond	*round*
zoet	*sweet*
snel	*fast*
saai	*boring*
smaken	*to taste*
fruitig	*fruity*
lekker	*nice*
vol	*full bodied*
licht	*light*
zwaar	*heavy*
zoet	*sweet*
kruidig	*spicy*
net	*neat and tidy*
saai	*boring*
ouderwets	*old fashioned*
hip	*hip*
modern	*modern*
fleurig	*colourful*
vrouwelijk	*feminine*
truttig	*dowdy*
opvallend	*striking*
goedkoop	*cheap*
duur	*expensive*
schoon	*clean*
conservatief	*conservative*
progressief	*progressive*
tolerant	*tolerant*
agressief	*aggressive*
dik	*fat*
slank	*slim*
aantrekkelijk	*attractive*
intelligent	*intelligent*
dom	*stupid*
stijf	*stiff*

New expressions

Ik heb zin in ...	*I fancy ...*
gevuld	*filled, stuffed*
een beetje	*a little bit*
duur	*expensive*
de loempia	*spring roll*
goedkoop	*cheap*
die	*they, those*
het dagmenu	*menu of the day*
de biefstuk	*steak*
Dat vind je toch ook lekker?	*You like that as well, don't you?*
minder gezond	*less healthy*
skeelerwedstrijd	*in-line skating competition*
die daar	*that one there*
stukken duurder	*much more expensive*
Wat maakt dat nou uit?	*So what?*
dan werk je toch een paar dagen meer in de zomer	*just work a few more days during the summer*
de vakantie	*holiday*
een glas wijn	*a glass of wine*
een Italiaanse maaltijd	*an Italian meal*
Chinees eten	*Chinese food*
een lange wandeling	*a long walk*
een belegd broodje	*a buttered roll with some sort of filling*
een warme zomer	*a warm summer*
een groot feest	*a big party*

Dialogue 1

At the delicatessen.

08.02 **Listen to the conversation. Do Wieteke and Gerrit decide to buy burritos or spring rolls?**

Wieteke	Wat zullen we nemen?
Gerrit	Ik heb zin in de gevulde burrito's vanavond.
Wieteke	Die zijn een beetje duur.
Gerrit	Hm ja. De loempia's zijn goedkoper. Zullen we die maar nemen?

Dialogue 2

In the restaurant.

08.03 **Listen to the conversation. Is Wieteke encouraging Gerrit to order the steak or the dish of the day?**

Wieteke	Neem jij het dagmenu?
Gerrit	Ik heb eigenlijk zin in biefstuk, maar dat is minder gezond.
Wieteke	Dan neem je het dagmenu toch? Dat vind je toch ook lekker?

> **LANGUAGE TIP**
>
> You have come across the word **toch** when it was used to check that your assumption is correct. Little words like **toch** are tricky in the sense that they can sometimes mean completely different things in different contexts. In the dialogue it is used to encourage Gerrit to order the dish of the day.

Dialogue 3

Mark and Tony are buying t-shirts for a skating competition.

08.04 **Listen to the conversation. Does Tony like the cheaper t-shirt?**

Mark	Jee, wat een cool T-shirt!
Tony	Nee joh. Die daar is toch veel hipper?
Mark	Ja, en ook stukken duurder.
Tony	Ach man, wat maakt dat nou uit? Dan werk je toch een paar dagen meer in de zomer?

Language discovery

The last dialogue contains many little words which frequently cannot be translated in an exact manner. These words can change the meaning of a sentence: they can indicate a certain tone, or they serve to indicate a certain relationship, e.g. a bond between friends.

jee	*gee*
nee joh	**joh** remains untranslated, but serves to create a sense of a bond between friends, like the word *man* in English
ach	*oh*
man	used to address a male person in a very colloquial manner
ach man	*"chill out, man"* is an example of *"man"*, though it's given next to *"ach man"*
toch	used here to help to convince

MAKING COMPARISONS

In the first dialogue in this unit Wieteke and Gerrit are deciding what to buy; in doing so, they are comparing prices of food. The word they use here for comparing is **goedkoper** *cheaper*.

In Unit 4 you were introduced to words that describe things and people – adjectives. You also use these adjectives to compare things and people. To do that in Dutch you add **-er** to the adjective:

goedkoop	→	**goedkoper**
klein	→	**kleiner**

Note the spelling change. However, you may have noticed that **duur** received an extra **d**. Adjectives ending with **r** get a **d** added before **-er**, thus: **duurder**.

Note that there are a few words which don't follow the same pattern.
These are:

goed	→	**beter**	*good*	→ *better*
veel	→	**meer**	*many*	→ *more*
weinig	→	**minder**	*few/little*	→ *less/fewer*

Also frequently used is:

graag	→	**liever**

Ik skeeler graag in m'n eentje.	*I like to go in-line skating on my own.*
Maar Jan skeelert liever in een groep.	*But Jan prefers to go in-line skating in a group.*

If you compare two things directly you must add the word **dan** (*than*):

Een Ford Galaxy is groter dan een Ferrari.

Deze bananen zijn bruiner dan die bananen.

Dit huis is groter dan dat huis.

Deze CD is duurder dan die.

Dit schilderij is mooier dan dat.

Repeating the word at the end sounds a little laborious, so you can normally leave it out

Dit T-shirt is cooler dan dat.

Look at this table which shows you when to use **dit** or **deze**, **dat** or **die**:

	het *word*	**de** *word*
this/these	**dit**	**deze**
that/those	**dat**	**die**

> **LANGUAGE TIP**
>
> With comparisons, strictly speaking, the word **dan** should be used. However, more and more Dutch speakers are using **als** instead. However, particularly in more formal situations, this can be seen as a very bad grammatical mistake. **Mijn hond is liever als jouw hond** (*My dog is sweeter than your dog*).

Practice

1 Look at this list:

Mevrouw Dijkstal	**een groot feest**
Erwin	**een Italiaanse maaltijd**
Pieter	**de vakantie**
Meneer Paardekoper	**een lange wandeling**

   a Make up mini-dialogues and ask each of these people what they fancy and give their responses. Write them down. Think about the correct register.

   b Write down for each of these people what they fancy. For example: **Mevrouw Dijkstal heeft zin in een groot feest.**

2 Answer the following questions and put the words between brackets in the correct form. For example:

Welke bloemen (flowers) wil je?

Ik vind die blauwe _____ (mooi). → *Ik vind die blauwe mooier.*

   a Wie vraag (ask) je op je feestje, Hans of Margaret?
      Hans, denk ik. Ik vind hem _____ (aardig).

   b Welke appels vind je lekker? De rode of de groene?
      Ik vind de rode _____ (lekker). De groene zijn _____ (zuur) (sour).

   c Welke koekjes wil je? Deze of die?
      Ik vind de ronde koekjes _____ (lekker). Die zijn _____ (zoet).

   d Welke auto wil je hebben? Een Ford Galaxy of een Ferrari?
      Een Ford Galaxy is _____ (groot), maar een Ferrari is _____ (snel).

   e Wat doe je liever? Skeeleren of schaatsen?
      Skeeleren vind ik _____ (leuk).

3 Complete using die or dat. Fill in the correct form of the word between brackets. For example:

Wil je in die stoel zitten?

Nee, _____ stoel zit _____ (lekker). → *Nee, deze stoel zit lekkerder.*

   a Vind je dit boek moeilijk?
      Nee, ik vind _____ boek _____ (moeilijk).

   b Vind je deze gele broek mooi?
      Nee, ik vind _____ rode broek _____ (mooi).

c Wil je deze krant hebben?

Nee, ik vind _____ krant _____ (interessant).

d Vind je dit artikel saai?

Nee, ik vind _____ artikel _____ (saai).

4 Compare these pictures and write sentences comparing these people. For example:

Lex is kleiner dan meneer Heeringa.

Meneer Heeringa is langer dan Lex.

Lex   meneer Heeringa

klein   lang

vrolijk (*cheerful*)   **verdrietig/depressief**

optimistisch (*optimistic*)

pessimistisch (*pessimistic*)

jong   oud

modern   **ouderwets** (*old fashioned*)

5 You are talking with a friend about the dress sense of two of your colleagues. Use the words in the following box. For example:

Jane's kleren zijn vrouwelijker dan die van Els.

Jane's clothes are more feminine than Els's.

6 Write a comparison of two major public figures. They could be sporting heroes, political figures or members of the royal family. Use adjectives you already know and some from this list in your description.

7 Practise comparing things by choosing two objects, pieces of furniture, houses or paintings.

? Test yourself

1 Wat heb je liever? Say which of the following pairs you prefer, following the example.

Example: rode wijn – bier. Answer: *Ik heb liever bier dan rode wijn.*

- **a** appels – sinaasappels
- **b** patat – salade
- **c** koffie – kruidenthee
- **d** aardappels – rijst
- **e** een frikadel – een kroket

2 Make comparisons of people you know, using the pairs given.

Example: lang – klein. Answer: *Mijn vriend Peter is langer dan mijn vriendin Johanna.* Or: *Mijn vriendin Johanna is kleiner dan mijn vriend Peter.*
(The answer depends on the people you know, of course.)

- **a** dik – dun
- **b** rijk – arm
- **c** saai – interessant
- **d** jong – oud
- **e** modern – ouderwets

SELF CHECK

I CAN ...
... compare things.

9 Ogenblikje, ik verbind u even door

Hold on a moment,

I'll just put you through

In this unit you will learn how to:
▶ *arrange to meet somewhere.*
▶ *have a telephone conversation.*

CEFR: (A2) *Can make arrangements to meet, decide where to go and what to do.*

Phone calls

When you answer the phone in the Netherlands you always answer with your name, as it is considered impolite to answer with just *hello*?

You can use either of the following two patterns: **met** (plus your name) or **U spreekt met** (plus your name). However, this last one is very formal.

There are various ways of saying *goodbye* in Dutch. You can say **tot zo** and **tot straks**, which both mean *see you in a little while*. If you did not know when you would meet again, you could say **tot ziens**. Similarly, if you knew you would meet again in the evening or the next morning, you could have said **tot vanavond**, **tot morgen** or **tot dan** (*see you then*).

A very informal way of saying *goodbye* is **doeg** and its variation **doei**, or even the Anglicism **ik zie je** (lit. *I see you*). Thanks to the influence of English, expressions such as *bye bye* and *see you* are used as well.

How would you answer the phone politely in Dutch?

Vocabulary builder

09.01 Listen to the new words and expressions.

het station	station
tot straks	see you later (lit. *till later*)
de trein	train
komt … aan (aankomen)	to arrive
haal … af (afhalen)	to pick up
tot zo	see you in a bit
de vlucht	the flight
het vliegveld	the airport
bedankt	thanks
NS (Nederlandse Spoorwegen)	the name of the Dutch Railways
reist	travel
gemakkelijk	easily
van en naar	from and to
reis	journey
én	and (the accent adds emphasis)
tegen een vast tarief	at a fixed rate
aantrekkelijk	attractive
boekt	book
van tevoren	beforehand
pas achteraf	not until afterwards
automatische incasso	direct debit
eerste	first
nog	another
meenemen	take along
per rit	per ride
thuis	at/from home
staat … klaar	is/will be waiting
de afspraak	the appointment
afspreken	to arrange (to meet), to make an appointment
uitkomen	to suit
helaas	unfortunately
afzeggen	cancel
een andere keer	another time
Komt morgen je goed uit?	Does tomorrow suit you?
beter	better
thuis	at home

weer	*again*
de afdeling	*department*
Personeelszaken	*personnel*
ogenblikje	*one moment, please*
verbind … door (doorverbinden)	*to put through (by phone)*
de praktijk	*(doctor's) practice*
de afdeling leningen	*loans department*
weggaan	*to go away*
meekomen	*to come along*
thuisblijven	*to stay at home*
ophangen	*to hang up*
meebrengen	*to bring along*
schoonmaken	*to clean*
uitgeven	*to spend*
afmaken	*to finish*
trouwens	*besides*

Dialogue 1

Linda is phoning Marijke on her mobile.

 09.02 Listen to the conversation and answer the questions.

1 What time does Linda's train arrive in Amersfoort?

Marijke	Met Marijke Smit.
Linda	Hallo, met Linda.
Marijke	O hallo, waar ben je?
Linda	Ik sta op het station en neem straks de trein van half zes. De trein komt om vijf over zes in Amersfoort aan. Haal je me dan van het station op?
Marijke	Goed, ik kom je zo ophalen.
Linda	Tot straks. Dag.
Marijke	Ja, tot zo.

2 09.03 Use the last dialogue to help you complete this conversation. You are about to embark on your flight to the Netherlands from Heathrow Airport and you phone your business partner there. You will need to use the Vocabulary builder.

Marco	Met Marco Haverhals.
You	*(Greet Marco and tell him who he is speaking with.)*
Marco	O hallo, waar ben je?
You	*(Tell him you are at Heathrow and that your flight is at 12.30 and arrives in Amsterdam at 14.30. Ask him if he can pick you up from the airport.)*
Marco	Goed, ik ben er om half 3.
You	*(Say thanks, see you later and goodbye.)*
Marco	Ja, tot dan. En een prettige reis.
You	*(Say see you then and have a good trip.)*

3 Answer the following questions.

  a What would they have said if they were going to meet again this afternoon?

  b And what would they have said if they were going to meet again on Sunday?

  c And on Wednesday?

  d And on Tuesday?

  e And what if they were going to meet again next week?

  f And next month?

Dialogue 2

Dinie phones Frouke, her homeopath.

09.04 Listen to the following conversation between Frouke and Dinie and answer the questions.

1 What does Frouke say when she answers the phone? Give the English translation.

Frouke	Met Frouke van den Broek.
Dinie	Dag Frouke, met Dinie Heijermans. Zeg, ik heb eigenlijk een afspraak met je voor maandag, maar ik moet die helaas afzeggen. Kan ik voor een andere keer afspreken?
Frouke	Ja, natuurlijk. Komt morgen je goed uit?
Dinie	Nee, dat komt mij niet zo goed uit. Donderdag is beter.
Frouke	Om tien uur?
Dinie	Ja dat is goed. Dan spreken we donderdag om tien uur af.
Frouke	Tot dan.
Dinie	Ja, tot dan.

2 Why does Dinie phone her homeopath?

3 Which expression indicates that Frouke readily agrees to this? Give the Dutch.

4 How does Frouke ask whether tomorrow will suit Dinie? Give the Dutch expression.

5 Does that suit Dinie?

6 When do they agree to meet?

 7 You phone the doctor because you have to cancel the appointment you made for Tuesday. Follow the prompts.

Doktersassistente	Met de praktijk van dokter de Boer.
You	*(Say who you are and that you have an appointment for tomorrow at 1.30 and that you regrettably have to cancel it – ask if you can arrange for a different time.)*
Doktersassistente	Even kijken. Komt donderdag u beter uit?
You	*(Say that Thursday doesn't suit you; ask if you can arrange for Wednesday.)*
Doktersassistente	Ja, woensdag kan. Om kwart voor drie?
You	*(Say yes and recap by saying that you would like to arrange it for Wednesday at 2.45.)*

Dialogue 3

 09.05 Listen to the following phone calls and answer the questions.

1 Where does Anja say that Bernard is?

Anja	Met Anja Heimans.
Peter	Dag Anja, met Peter. Is Berend thuis?
Anja	Hij is naar zijn moeder vandaag, maar hij is vanavond weer thuis.
Peter	Goed, ik bel hem vanavond wel.
Receptioniste	Met de afdeling Personeelszaken.
Peter	Kan ik met meneer de Haan spreken?
Receptioniste	Ogenblikje, ik verbind u even door.

2 Which two phrases are used on the phone to ask to talk to someone?

3 Ask if you can talk to meneer Plantinga.

4 Ask if Menno is at home.

5 09.06 Make up dialogues for the following situations.

  a You phone your friend Alice. Her husband, Dirk Jansen, answers the phone and says that Alice is at a party, but that she will be home tomorrow. You say you will phone tomorrow.

  b You phone the loans department of your local bank. You ask for Mrs Blom and the girl who answers the phone says she will put you through.

Language discovery

DAG

09.07 Dag is another way of saying *goodbye*. However, it is also used for *hello*. When **dag** is used as a greeting, then the pronunciation is short. Practise this:

dag, Arend	**dag, Richard**
dag, Ineke	**dag, Carol**

When **dag** is used as *goodbye*, it is normally pronounced with an extended '**ah**' sound as in '**dahag**'. Practise this:

tot ziens	**tot straks**
dag (dahag)	**dag (dahag)**

Read the advertisement for the NS Zonetaxi and answer the questions in Dutch.

> Met NS Zonetaxi reist u gemakkelijk en snel van en naar het station.
>
> Maak van uw treinreis een comfortabele deur-tot-deur-reis met de Zonetaxi van NS. Hiermee reist u gemakkelijk én snel van en naar het station tegen een aantrekkelijk vast tarief per zone.
>
> U boekt een taxi tot 30 minuten van tevoren via internet of mobiele telefoon. U betaalt pas achteraf via automatische incasso. De minimum prijs is zes euro voor de eerste zone. U kunt nog drie personen meenemen per rit. De taxi haalt u thuis op of staat op het station klaar.

a Hoe reis je met NS Zonetaxi van en naar het station?
b Wat is het tarief voor NS Zonetaxi?
c Hoe boek je NS Zonetaxi?
d Hoe betaal je?
e Hoeveel personen kun je meenemen?

SEPARABLE VERBS

Go back to the first two dialogues in this unit and look at the verbs **afhalen** and **afspreken**. Sometimes these verbs appear as here, but sometimes they appear split into two parts. These verbs where the first part can be split from the main part are called **separable verbs**. When we want to use these verbs as the main verb (action word) in the sentence, the first part splits away and appears at the end of the sentence. For example:

Hij zegt onze afspraak voor morgen af.	*He's cancelling our appointment for tomorrow.*
De trein komt om half elf aan.	*The train arrives at half past ten.*
We spreken om 3 uur af.	*We arrange to meet at 3 o'clock.*

Ik haal je straks af.	*I'll pick you up in a minute.*
Ik verbind u door.	*Putting you through.*
Het komt me goed uit.	*That will suit me.*

As you can see, the main part of the verb behaves according to the rules set out in Unit 1.

In Unit 7 we saw that it is possible to use more than one verb in a sentence. This is also possible with separable verbs. When the separable verb is used with another verb, such as **zullen** or **willen**, then it behaves according to the rules set out in Unit 7 and goes to the end of the sentence. This means that the main part of the separable verb meets up with its first part at the end of the sentence. For example:

Ik zal om half zes aankomen.	*I'll arrive at half past five.*
Zullen we voor morgen afspreken?	*Shall we arrange to meet tomorrow?*
Ik kom je afhalen.	*I'll come and pick you up.*

> **LANGUAGE TIP**
>
> **Mee** means along or with, and can be used to make up lots of different separable verbs. Some examples: **meegaan** (*to go along*), **Ga je ook mee?** (*Are you going along too?*); **meezingen** (*to sing along*), **Iedereen zingt mee** (*Everyone is singing along*); **meedoen** (*to join in, lit. to do along*), **België doet mee aan de reddingsactie** (*Belgium is joining the rescue operation*).

Practice

1 **Answer the following questions in the affirmative using the separable verb. For example:**

Zullen we nu weggaan?

Ja, we gaan nu weg.

NB Think about the correct forms of the verbs as well as the correct pronouns (**wij**, **jullie**, **ik**, etc.). For example:

Moeten jullie het werk nog afmaken? *(Do you still have to finish your work?)*

Ja, we maken het werk nog af.

   a Willen jullie morgen meekomen?
   b Willen jullie graag thuisblijven?
   c Ga jij het schilderij in de kamer ophangen?
   d Wil jij de pizza meebrengen?
   e Wil jij het huis schoonmaken?

2 **Ask the same questions substituting Peter en Dries for** jullie **and substitute Lena for** jij. **Answer the questions as well. For example:**

Willen Peter en Dries morgen meekomen?

Ja, zij komen morgen mee.

3 09.08 **You are phoning your friend Harry and you suggest doing something the next day. You have to negotiate to come to a compromise. You need to use various structures and words which you have learnt so far. Write down your part first and then act it out either by reading both parts out loud or with the audio.**

Harry	Met Harry Donkers.
You	*(Greet Harry, say who you are and suggest going to play football the next day.)*
Harry	Ik heb daar eigenlijk geen zin in. Trouwens, ik moet morgen werken.
You	*(Suggest going to the cinema on Saturday evening.)*
Harry	Ja, daar heb ik wel zin in.
You	*(Ask what time you should arrange to meet.)*
Harry	Kun je om kwart over zeven bij mij zijn?
You	*(Say that's OK and you'll see him on Saturday.)*

LANGUAGE TIP

Make sure you don't mistake Dutch **bij** to mean English *by*. **Bij** means *at* or *near*. So **Kom je bij mij eten?** means *Are you coming to mine for dinner?* And when someone calls you to ask where you are, you might answer: **Bij mijn ouders** (*At my parents*).

Test yourself

1 Give two ways of saying *See you later* in Dutch.

2 If you're saying goodbye to someone who you'll see again in the afternoon, what could you say?

3 Give two different ways of greeting someone.

4 What would you say if you were answering the phone in Dutch?

5 You're calling Simon. His girlfriend Petra answers the phone. Ask Petra if Simon is at home.

6 Use the verb **afspreken** to tell a friend that your are arranging to meet tomorrow at a quarter to two.

7 Translate the following sentences, using the verbs in brackets:
   a I am going to finish my work. (afmaken)
   b I'll pick you up at half past six. (ophalen)
   c Jean arrives at five o'clock. (aankomen)
   d We are staying at home tonight. (thuisblijven)

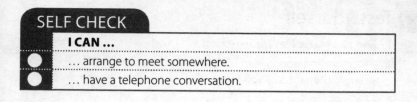

10 Kom binnen
Come in

In this unit you will learn how to:
▶ *give and follow instructions.*
▶ *understand recipes.*
▶ *talk about the environment.*

CEFR: (B1) *Can give detailed instructions.*

 ## Using commands

We use commands and orders more often than you think, and usually in friendlier situations than the name itself suggests. For instance, in a restaurant or shop the waiter or sales person may tell you **zegt u het maar** (lit. *say it*) when it's your turn to order or say what you want to buy.

The environment

In order to live an environmentally friendly lifestyle, more and more people **recyclen** (*to recycle*) their **afval** (*waste*), which is common throughout Belgium and the Netherlands. And to save energy, for instance, increasingly people are using **spaarlampen** (*energy saving light bulbs*).

What do you think **spaar** in **spaarlampen** means?

Vocabulary builder

binnen	*inside*
buiten	*outside*
koud	*cold*
oppassen	*to look after*
stilzitten	*to sit still*
het afval	*rubbish*
organisch	*organic*
wegwerp	*disposable*
de glasbak	*bottle bank*
scheiden	*to separate*
tweedehands	*secondhand*
meubels	*furniture*
(weg)gooien	*to throw away*
de vuilniszak	*rubbish bag*
inleveren	*to hand in*
chemisch	*chemical (adj.)*
de Chemokar	*council vehicle that comes and collects chemical*
waste	*from special locations*
meteen	*immediately*
spullen	*things*
het ding	*thing*
repareren	*to repair*
kapot	*broken*
gebruiken	*to use*
eigen	*own*
doe het licht uit	*switch the light off*
als het niet nodig	*is if it isn't needed*
de lijst	*list*
de boter	*butter*
de koekepan	*frying pan*
plakje	*slice*
het ei (plural: eieren)	*egg*
de augurk	*gherkin*
snijden	*to cut*
de boterham	*slice of bread, sandwich*
smeren	*to butter*

bovenop	on top
leggen	to put
Eet smakelijk!	Enjoy your meal!
makkelijk	easy
sparen	to save
energie	energy
de verwarming lager zetten	to turn the heating down
leeg	empty
het idee	idea
isoleren	to insulate
af en toe	now and then
het raam	window
gebruikt meer water	uses more water
op de knop drukken	press the button/switch off an appliance

Dia logue

10.02 Listen to the following short exchanges and note the different tones of voice with which these invitations are uttered. Choose from the following list of words to describe each of the situations.

1 invite directly
2 irritable
3 permissive
4 to encourage

NB There may be more than one possibility.

a *Wilma is expecting her friend and invites her in.*

Wilma   Hallo, kom binnen.
Doe je jas uit.
Ga zitten.

b *When a friend of Wilma's son, Robert, comes round to give Robert something, Wilma says:*

Wilma   Hallo, kom maar even binnen.

c *Mirjam is sitting with her son in a waiting room. It is hot and she says:*

Mirjam   Doe je jas maar uit.

d *Wilma says to Sietske and Jan who are standing chatting outside her front door:*

Wilma   Kom toch binnen, het is koud buiten.

e *Wilma says to Sietske who is standing in the living room with her coat on:*

Wilma   Doe je jas toch uit.

f *When Sietske is still standing, she says:*

Wilma   Ga toch zitten.

Language discovery

ORDERS, INSTRUCTIONS AND INVITATIONS

Strictly speaking, the patterns you have just seen are commands or orders. The way in which words are said plus the situation in which they are said determine whether they are meant as an order, an instruction or an invitation. Also the addition of words like **maar** and **toch** can change the intention of the sentence.

The addition of **maar** changes the command into an invitation or encouragement. **Kom maar met ons mee** sounds more gentle and encouraging than **Kom met ons mee**.

Schiet toch op.   *Do hurry.*

The addition of **toch** assumes that there was a delay. It could even sound as if the speaker were a little irritated, although that is not always necessarily the case.

Orders can also be used for different reasons, for instance, to encourage people to carry out certain actions or to give advice:

Geniet van wijnen uit de Provence! *Enjoy wines from Provence!*

Koop nu uw nieuwe mobiel! *Buy a new mobile phone now!*

Ga naar huis, je bent moe. *Go home, you are tired.*

You have come across orders and commands before in sentences such as **Geef mij maar een pilsje**. The patterns of orders and commands in this unit are formed in the same way. For example:

Doe de deur dicht. *Close the door.*

Ga naar binnen. *Go inside.*

Klik op de muis. *Click on the mouse.*

In these orders the person who is addressed is not actually directly referred to in the sentence, i.e. the words **jij** or **u** are not used.

Look at the actual verbs in these commands. They all have the same form, namely the stem of the verb. (This is the verb with the **-en** or **-n** taken off the end.) Naturally this is adjusted for spelling:

zitten becomes **zit** **geven** becomes **geef**

eten becomes **eet** **gaan** becomes **ga**

Can you change the following questions into orders? For example:

Kun je de deur dichtdoen? → *Doe de deur dicht.*

  a Kun je straks de boodschappen doen?
  b Kun je me vanavond bellen?
  c Kun je deze les voor morgen leren?
  d Wil je oom Jan vanavond schrijven?
  e Kun je dit artikel lezen?
  f Wil je niet zo hard schreeuwen?

Practice

1 Complete using toch or maar as appropriate.

  a Ga _____ naar huis. (colleague who is fed up with the secretary sneezing and spluttering over her desk)
  b Ga _____ naar huis. (boss, kindly, to secretary who is obviously ill)
  c Zit _____ stil. (mother to fidgety child)
  d Hou _____ je mond. (mother to her incessantly chatting child)
  e Doe het raam _____ open. (teacher gives child permission to open the window, because it is so warm)

f Doe het raam _____ open. (teacher to same child who is delaying opening the window)

g Ga _____ met Jantien uit vanavond. Ik pas wel op de kinderen. (husband encourages his wife to go out while he looks after the children)

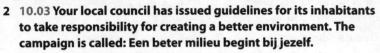

2 **10.03 Your local council has issued guidelines for its inhabitants to take responsibility for creating a better environment. The campaign is called: Een beter milieu begint bij jezelf.**
(*A better environment starts with you.*)

a Read the following advice from the council:

Koop geen melk in pakken, maar in flessen.

Scheid groenteafval van het gewone afval.

Gebruik een vulpen in plaats van een wegwerppen.

Breng uw flessen naar de glasbak.

Breng uw oud papier naar de papierbak.

Koop tweedehands meubels.

Gooi chemisch afval niet in de vuilniszak.

Lever uw chemisch afval in bij de Chemokar.

Breng uw oude kleren naar de tweedehands winkel. Koop niet meteen nieuwe spullen, maar repareer kapotte dingen.

Gebruik geen plastic tassen, maar neem uw eigen boodschappentas mee.

Doe het licht uit (als het niet nodig is).

Hang deze lijst in de keuken op.

b Read through the text thoroughly again and make sure you understand most of the words. Then answer the following questions about the text.

1 In what kind of containers do you need to buy milk?

2 What do you need to do with vegetable waste?

3 What kind of pen are you advised to write with?

4 What should you not do with chemical waste?

5 What are you advised to do with your old clothes?

6 You are advised not to buy too many new items. What are you supposed to do when old things break down?

c Read the text again and underline all the verbs that make up the instructions. Make sure you also include the split-up sections of the separable verbs (**inleveren**, **meenemen**, **uitdoen** and **ophangen** are separable verbs).

d You have just read this council list and you are now writing a letter to your friend who did not receive the leaflet. Tell your friend how to do his bit for the environment. Write down each of these sentences in full using the verb **moeten**. Don't forget that **uw** will change to **je**. For example:

Je moet geen melk in pakken kopen, maar in flessen.

Je moet groenteafval van het gewone afval scheiden.

Je moet je flessen naar de glasbak brengen.

3 10.04 **Listen to and read this recipe:**

Uitsmijter

U moet de boter in de koekepan doen.

U moet 3 plakjes ham in de koekepan bakken.

U moet 3 eieren in de pan doen.

U moet een augurk en een tomaat in plakjes snijden.

U moet 3 boterhammen smeren.

U moet de eieren, de ham, de plakjes tomaat en de augurk bovenop de boterham leggen.

Eet smakelijk!

Now change these full sentences into clear instructions. For example:

Doe de boter in de koekepan ...

4 **10.05 Listen to the broadcast with tips about energy saving. Using the letters on the drawing, indicate which recommendations were made. Use the pattern for instructions, e.g.** Zet de verwarming lager (*turn down the heating*). **You will have to refer to the Vocabulary builder. Remember, for an exercise like this you do not have to understand everything that is said, but you do need to learn to pick up the information that is relevant to you. Listen to the broadcast several times and you will find that gradually you understand more of what is said. The full text of the broadcast is printed in the Answer key.**

Test yourself

1 Some friends are coming over for dinner. You're welcoming them in Dutch. Follow the instructions.

   a They knock on the door. Greet them and invite them in.

   b Invite them to take their coat off.

   c Suggest that they sit down.

2 In the following sentences, does **maar** indicate that the speaker is being polite or irritated?

   a Geef je jas maar aan mij!

   b Kom maar met me mee.

3 In the following sentences, does **toch** indicate that the speaker is being polite or irritated?

   a Geef dat boek toch hier!

   b Kom toch met me mee.

4 Fill in **maar** or **toch**.

   a Je hebt al genoeg gedaan. Ga _____ naar huis. (your boss tells you that you can go home)

   b Blijf _____ stil zitten! (a father to his daughter, who has been annyoing him)

   c Drink je drankje _____ op. (a husband to his wife, at a party he wants to leave)

   d Geef mij _____ een biertje. (your answer to your host's question what you'd like to drink)

SELF CHECK

I CAN ...
... give and follow instructions.
... understand recipes.
... talk about the environment.

Answer key

Disovery question: No. If you know someone well, you can address them as je or jij.

Vocabulary builder: German; Dutch; Italian; **1** vrouw; **2** Ik spreek Nederlands.

Text: 1 Hij is docent; **2** Zij spreekt Nederlands; Hij spreekt Duits

Language Discovery: 1 a Ik ben Karel Bos. Ik ben zakenman. Ik spreek Engels en Frans. Ik woon in Amsterdam. Ik help Jill Johnson. **b** Ik ben Tom Peters. Ik ben docent. Ik spreek Engels en Spaans. Ik woon in Utrecht. Ik help Allie Mitchel; **2 a** Ik ben Gail Boonstra. Ik ben computerprogrammeur. Ik spreek Nederlands en Engels. Ik woon in Edam. Ik werk bij een bedrijf. **b** Ik ben Ad Visser. Ik ben manager. Ik spreek alleen Nederlands. Ik woon in Zutphen. Ik werk bij/in een winkel; **3** het; zij; zij; **4** ik denk, jij denkt, u denkt, hij/zij/het denkt, wij denken, jullie denken, u denkt, zij denken; ik drink, jij drinkt, u drinkt, hij/zij/het drinkt, wij drinken, jullie drinken, u drinkt, zij drinken; **5** they are the same

Listen and speak: a U bent mevrouw Schipper? **b** Jij bent Wim Den Uyl? **c** Jij bent Joop Tersteeg? **d** U bent meneer Brink.

Practice 1: 1 Jij bent (toch) Sara Bakker (hè)?, Jij bent (toch) verpleegster (hè)?, Jij spreekt (toch) Engels en Frans (hè)?, Jij woont (toch) in Hilversum (hè)? Jij helpt (toch) Ben Mendoza (hè)? Jij werkt (toch) in een ziekenhuis (hè)?; Jij bent (toch) Leona Beke (hè)? Jij bent (toch) bankassistente (hè)? Jij spreekt (toch) Engels en Italiaans (hè)? Jij woont (toch) in Amersfoort (hè)? Jij helpt (toch) Marisa Delporte (hè)? **2** Mevrouw Schipper woont in Amersfoort. Joop Tersteeg en Marco Cohen wonen in Leeuwarden. Meneer Brink woont in Utrecht. **3** Saskia de Boer spreekt Engels en Duits. Ruud Krol spreekt Engels en Spaans. Sietske Zwart en Mark Cohen spreken Engels en Russisch.

Go further: verpleger verpleegster = nurse; administrateur administratrice = administrator; architect architect = architect

Practice 2: 1 a Hij is winkelbediende/ winkelassistent. **b** Hij is tandarts. **c** Zij is studente. **d** Zij is kunstenares. **e** Hij is website-ontwerper. **f** Zij is bankassistente. **g** Hij is architect. **h** Zij is administratrice/secretaresse. **i** Hij is acteur; **2 a** Amsterdam. **b** Vlaanderen. **c** Alkmaar. **d** Den Haag. **e** Brussel. **f** Maastricht. **g** Arnhem. **h** Haarlem. **i** de Waddenzee. **j** Rotterdam. **k** Antwerpen. **l** Hilversum. **m** Groningen.

Unit 2

Discovery question: hoi

Vocabulary builder: good afternoon; what do you do?

Dialogue 1: What is your name?

Expressions 1: 1c because Ms Droog address Ms Pruim by her surname, and greets her with 'good afternoon'.

2 a Goedemiddag, (dag) mevrouw Dekker. Hoe gaat het? Het gaat goed, dank u. **b** Dag Henk. Hoe gaat het? (alles goed?) Het gaat niet zo goed. ('t kan beter) **c** Dag, Jan. (Hoi, Jan) Hoe gaat het? Ach, het gaat wel. ('t gaat, 't gaat) **d** Goedenavond, (dag) meneer Kok. Hoe gaat het? Het gaat uitstekend. Dank u.

Dialogue 2: 1 Haarlem; **2** Amsterdam

Dialogue 3: 1 No, in Blasiusstraat; **2** Jan works in Utrecht

Language discovery 2: 1 a Waar woon jij? Ik woon in Leeuwarden. **b** Waar wonen Frans en Mieke? Zij wonen in Rotterdam. **c** Waar woont Janneke? Zij woont in Den Bosch. **d** Waar werk jij? Ik werk in Haarlem. **e** Waar werkt Karel? Hij werkt in Amsterdam. **f** Waar wonen jullie? Wij wonen in Groningen; **2 a** Wat doet u? Ik ben verpleegster. **b** Wat doe jij? Ik ben advocaat. **c** Wat doe jij? Ik ben docent. **d** Wat doet u? Ik ben dokter. **e** Wat doe jij? Ik ben redacteur.

3 a Wat drink jij? **b** Wat zoek jij? **c** Wat maak jij? **d** Wat schrijft u?

Dialogue 4: London

Language discovery 3: 1 a Waar is de w.c.? **b** Waar staat de koffie? **c** Waar zit Lieve? **d** Waar zit je?

Dialogue 5: 1 In the avenue of Osnabrüc avenue; **2** Go straight, then left

Dialogue 6: You go left, past the post office. It is on the right.

Dialogue 7: on the left.

Practice: a Waar is het ziekenhuis? Het ziekenhuis is aan de linkerkant. **b** Waar is het zwembad? Het zwembad is aan de linkerkant. **c** Waar is het station? Het station is aan de linkerkant. **d** Waar is het internetcafé ? Het internetcafé is aan de rechterkant. **e** Waar is het postkantoor?

Het postkantoor is aan de rechterkant. **f** Waar is het wisselkantoor? Het wisselkantoor is aan de rechterkant.

Test Yourself: 1 Waar werkt Karel? Hij werkt in Amsterdam; **2** Waar wonen jullie? Wij wonen in Groningen; **3 a** Wat vervelend! **b** Wat leuk! **c** Wat knap! **d** Wat interessant!/Wat mooi! **e** Wat leuk!

Unit 3

Discovery question: statiegeld

Vocabulary builder: cost; **2** NB These are examples only. Hoeveel kost de rode wijn? Hoeveel kosten de druiven? Hoeveel kost de spa blauw? Hoeveel kost een bolletje? Hoeveel kost de belegen kaas?

Dialogue 1: 1 6 euro; **2** 250 grammes

New Expressions: 1 a zeventien **b** negen acht zeven zes twee één **c** één één één negen; **2 a** twee plus elf is dertien **b** twintig min acht is twaalf **c** vier keer vier is zestien **d** drie keer vijf is vijftien **e** zeventien min negen is acht **f** zeven plus zes is dertien **g** achttien min vier is veertien **h** zes min zes is nul

Language Discovery 2: 1 a Er zijn nog tweeëndertig croissants. **b** Er zijn nog honderd vijfenzeventig flessen witte wijn. **c** Er zijn nog tweehonderd negenendertig flessen rode wijn. **d** Er zijn nog vierenzestig pakken melk. **e** Er zijn nog vijfennegentig kuipjes boter. **f** Er zijn nog achtenzeventig tubes tandpasta. **g** Er zijn nog honderd zestien plastic tasjes. **h** Er zijn nog tweeëntwintig kratten pils.

2 a Hoeveel kost de fles rode wijn? De fles rode wijn kost vier euro vijfentwintig. **b** Hoeveel kost de krat pils? De krat pils kost 11 euro 10. **c** Hoeveel kost het pak melk? Het pak melk kost 76 (euro)cent. **d** Hoeveel kosten de peren? De peren kosten 1 euro 88 per kilo. **e** Hoeveel kost de kaas? De kaas kost 3 euro 5 per kilo.

New Expressions 2: a Hoeveel sinaasappels heb je nodig? Ik heb vijf sinaasappels nodig. **b** Hoeveel pakken melk heb je nodig? Ik heb twee pakken (melk) nodig. **c** Hoeveel flessen bier heb je nodig? Ik heb twaalf flessen (bier) nodig. **d** Hoeveel bloemkolen heb je nodig? Ik heb één bloemkool nodig. **e** Hoeveel appels heb je nodig? Ik heb 1 kilo (appels) nodig. **f** Hoeveel pakken rijst heb je nodig? Ik heb vier pakken (rijst) nodig. **g** Hoeveel bonen heb je nodig? Ik heb twee kilo bonen nodig. **h** Hoeveel druiven heb je nodig? Ik heb een pond druiven nodig.

Language discovery 3: a appels, **b** vrouwen, **c** disco's, **d** flessen, **e** programma's, **f** computers, **g** grachten.

Dialogue 2 1 the young cheese; **2** Welke kaas wil je? Welke koekjes wil je? Welk brood wil je? Welke chips wil je? Welke chocola wil je? Welke drop wil je? Welk snoepje wil je?

Dialogue 3 1brown bread; **2** 4.50 euros

Unit 4

Discovery question: one brother each

Vocabulary builder: father; its

Dialogue 1: 1 reading the newspaper; **2** two tents; **3** her mother's brother

Practice 1: 1 Example sentences: Tante Nel en oom Arend zijn aardig. Mijn ooms zijn groot. Mijn zus is vervelend. Mijn broer is klein. Mijn zus en mijn broer zijn vervelend. Mijn dochter is mooi. Mijn vader is zakenman. Mijn moeder is dokter. Mijn man is lief. Mijn vrouw is mooi.

2 a zijn **b** zijn **c** haar **d** haar **e** zijn **f** haar

Dialogue 2: 1 long black boots, a short red skirt and a tight blouse; **2** a shirt and tie; **3** sporty clothes

Practice 2: 1 a Ik draag mijn witte T-shirt, mijn blauwe spijkerbroek, mijn rode jas en mijn gele petje. **b** Ik draag een witte rok, een blauw T-shirt, een rode trui en een gele bril. **c** Hij draagt een witte broek, een blauw colbert, een rood overhemd en een gele hoed. **4 a** Ik hou van witte wijn. **b** Jij houdt van rode wijn, hè? **c** Jantien houdt van zwarte kleren. **d** Mijn ouders houden van grote huizen. **e** Mijn kinderen houden van oranje voetbalshirts. **f** Mandy houdt van kleine kinderen; **5 a 1** vader, moeder, oma, opa **2** zus, vriendin **3** vader, zoon **4** opa, oma, moeder, vader, oom, tante, zus **b 1** oma – grote hoed; opa – bril **2** zus – rood T-shirt; vriendin – gele broek **3** vader – net pak; zoon – rugzak **4** oom Piet – stropdas; tante Katy – groene jurk

Go Further 1 a Jasmijn houdt van wijn. Zij draagt een broek en een jas. Zij draagt een bril. Zij heeft drie kinderen. **b** Jaap houdt van sportieve kleren. Hij draagt een spijkerbroek. Hij houdt van bier. Hij heeft een computer.

3 a Jolanda: sexy, but wears a very short skirt; Willem-Alexander: is very tall and good- looking; Frédérique: is always late and moody; Jos: doesn't work very hard and goes home early.

Here's the text of the dialogues: **I A:** Daar is Jolanda. **B:** Goh, zij is sexy! **A:** Ja, maar haar rok is wel erg kort; **II A:** Kijk, dat is Willem-Alexander. **B:** Wat is hij lang, zeg! **A:** Ja, en ook erg knap. **B:** Vind je?; **III A:** Waar is Frédérique? **B:** Ik weet het niet. **A:** Ze is altijd te laat. **B:** Ja, inderdaad. En ze is altijd zo chagrijnig; **IV A:** Is dat Jos? **B:** Ja, hij werkt samen met Jolanda. Hij werkt alleen niet echt hard. **A:** Oh, echt? **B:** Mm, en hij gaat vaak nogal vroeg naar huis

Unit 5

Discovery question: met mean with, patat met literally means potatoes with

Dialogue 1: 1 a glass of red wine; **2 a** Ik wil graag een (glas) sinaasappelsap; een sinaasappelsap, graag. **b** Ik wil graag een limonade; een limonade, graag. **c** Ik wil graag een borrel; een borrel, graag. **d** Ik wil graag een glas fris; een glas fris, graag. **e** Ik wil graag een cassis; een cassis, graag. **f** Ik wil graag een kopje thee met melk en (met) suiker; een kopje thee met melk en suiker, graag. **g** Ik wil graag een kopje koffie met melk en zonder suiker; een kopje koffie met melk en zonder suiker, graag. **h** Ik wil graag een (glas) ananassap; een (glas) ananassap, graag; **3** chips; **4.** No, she asks for a vodka; **5 a** The dialogue with Berend and Annie. **b** The use of 'u' instead of 'je/jij'. Longer and more complete sentences. More polite by using polite phrases, e.g. mag ik een …, ik wil graag … there is more distance between the speakers in the formal dialogue. Chantal is using an informal phrase for ordering a drink. She is also trying to personalise the contact with the waiter by asking if he has a nice drink for her. That way she is drawing attention to their 'relationship'; **6** Berend, Annie en de kinderen zitten in een restaurant. Ze hebben dorst en ze bestellen iets te drinken. Berend wil een pilsje, maar Annie neemt een jus d'orange. Ze hebben ook honger. Berend en Annie nemen een uitsmijter, maar ze bestellen patat voor de kinderen. Chantal zit in een café. Ze wil een lekker drankje. Ze bestelt een wodka.

Practice: 1 a Mag ik een glas witte wijn? Geeft u mij maar een glas witte wijn. Een glas witte wijn, graag. Doe maar een glas witte wijn. **b** Mag ik een kopje thee? Geeft u mij maar een kopje thee. Een kopje thee, graag. Doe maar een kopje thee. **c** Mag ik een uitsmijter? Geeft u mij maar een uitsmijter. Een uitsmijter, graag. Doe maar een uitsmijter. **d** Mag ik een jenever? Geeft u mij maar een jenever. Een jenever, graag. Doe maar een jenever. **e** Mag ik een (glas) druivensap? Geeft u mij maar een druivensap. Een druivensap, graag. Doe maar een druivensap. **f** Mag ik een stuk appeltaart? Geeft u mij maar een stuk appeltaart. Een stuk appeltaart, graag. Doe maar een stuk appeltaart. **g** Mag ik een slaatje? Geeft u mij maar een slaatje. Een slaatje, graag. Doe maar een slaatje. **h** Mag ik een pizza? Geeft u mij maar een pizza. Een pizza, graag. Doe maar een pizza. **2 a** Mag ik een fles witte wijn? **b** Doe maar een spa rood. **c** Een vruchtensap, graag. **d** Doe maar een bruin bolletje met geitenkaas en tijm. **e** Geeft u mij maar aspergesoep. **f** Doe maar een tonijnsalade. **g** Mag ik de vegetarische schotel? **h** Doe maar de dagschotel.

Language discovery: a haar **b** mij **c** hen **d** ons **e** jou **f** hem. **7** haar, mij, hem, ze/hen.

Unit 6

Discovery question: een tent or een caravan, or perhaps huisjes or trekkershutten

Language discovery 1:1 a Ik ben Amerikaans. **b** Ik ben Frans. **c** Ik ben Iers. **d** Ik ben Chinees. **e** Ik ben Schots. **f** Ik ben Duits; **2 a** Nederlandse **b** Amerikaanse **c** Schotse **d** Duits **e** Italiaanse **f** Spaanse **g** Ierse **h** Britse.

Dialogue: 1 two nights; **2** Het huisje kost 30 euro per nacht (30 euros per night) **3** Dennis komt uit Engeland (from England) **4** Het adres van Dennis in Nederland is: Burgweg 35 in Papendrecht **5** Het telefoonnummer van Dennis is 00 44 7953 774326

Language discovery 2: a Nee, ik boek de tickets niet. Ik heb het te druk. **b** Nee, ik bestel de taxi niet. Ik heb het druk. **c** Nee, ik organiseer de excursies niet. Ik heb het te druk. **d** Nee, ik pak de koffers niet. Ik heb het te druk. **e** Nee, ik koop de malariapillen niet. Ik heb het te druk. **f** Nee, ik wissel het geld niet. Ik heb het te druk.

Practice 1: a Ja, ik hou van moderne kleren. Nee, ik hou niet van moderne kleren. **b** Ja, ik hou van grote tuinen. Nee, ik hou niet van grote tuinen. **c** Ja, ik werk in Groningen. Nee, ik werk niet in Groningen. **d** Ja, ik woon in Amersfoort. Nee, ik woon niet in Amersfoort. **e** Ja, mijn schoenen zijn oud. Nee, mijn schoenen zijn niet oud. **f** Ja, ik drink graag thee zonder melk. Nee, ik drink niet graag thee zonder melk. **g** Ja, ik ben de nieuwe manager. Nee, ik ben de nieuwe manager niet. **h** Ja, de bananen zijn duur. Nee, de bananen zijn niet duur. **i** Ja, ik ga naar mijn werk. Nee, ik ga niet naar mijn werk. **j** Ja, dit is mijn jas. Nee, dit is mijn jas niet.

Language discovery 3: a Nee, ik drink geen melk. **b** Nee, ik koop geen appels. **c** Nee, ik eet geen chocola. **d** Nee, ik spreek geen Frans. **e** Nee ik heb geen kinderen. **f** Nee, ik neem geen uitsmijter. **g** Nee, ik wil geen slaatje. **h** Nee, ik breng geen pizza.

Practice 2: 2 En jij? Werk jij of studeer je? Ik werk. Ik ben docent op een school in Amsterdam. Werk je daar al lang? Sinds twee jaar; **3 a** Nee, ik luister niet naar de radio. **b** Nee, ik ga niet naar restaurants. **c** Nee, ik ga niet naar feesten. **d** Nee, ik drink geen wijn.

e Nee, ik spreek geen Frans. **f** Nee, ik eet geen pizza's. **g** Nee, ik draag geen spijkerbroeken; **4** Peter Bos, politieagent, Nederlands, Alkmaar, 1824TB, 072 5689 701.

Unit 7

Dialogue 1: 1 No, he doesn't think it is interesting; **2 a** Ik ga morgen de school opbellen. **b** Ik ga morgen schaatsen. **c** Ik ga morgen zwemmen. **d** Ik ga morgen in een restaurant eten; **3 a** Moet je morgen boodschappen doen? Ja, ik moet morgen boodschappen doen. **b** Moet je morgen jouw huis schilderen? Ja, ik moet morgen mijn huis schilderen. **c** Moet je morgen je vriend e-mailen? Ja, ik moet morgen mijn vriend e-mailen. **d** Moet je morgen schoonmaken? Ja, ik moet morgen schoonmaken.

Dialogue 3: 1 No; **2 a** Ga je morgen de school bellen? Nee, ik ga morgen de school niet bellen, maar ik ga dansen. **b** Ga je morgen schaatsen? Nee, ik ga morgen niet schaatsen, maar ik ga dansen. **c** Ga je morgen zwemmen? Nee, ik ga morgen niet zwemmen, maar ik ga dansen. **d** Ga je morgen fietsen? Nee, ik ga morgen niet fietsen, maar ik ga dansen. **e** Ga je morgen in een restaurant eten? Nee, ik ga morgen niet in een restaurant eten, maar ik ga dansen.

Practice 1: 1 Dinsdag gaat hij boodschappen doen. Woensdag gaat Jeroen schoonmaken. Donderdag gaat hij Janine bellen. Vrijdag gaat hij dansen. Zaterdag gaat Jeroen voetballen. Zondag gaat hij zijn ouders bezoeken. **2 a** Ga je overmorgen dansen? **b** Ga je vanavond sporten? **c** Ga je volgende week werken? **d** Ga je vanmiddag boodschappen doen? **e** Ga je volgend jaar jouw huis schilderen?

Practice 2: 1 a Ik ben niet geïnteresseerd in moderne kunst. **b** Ik ben niet geïnteresseerd in politiek. **c** Ik ben niet geïnteresseerd in science fiction. **d** Ik ben niet geïnteresseerd in sport. **e** Ik ben niet geïnteresseerd in popmuziek; **2 a** Ik ben geïnteresseerd in klassieke muziek. **b** Ik ben geïnteresseerd in Nederlandse literatuur. **c** Ik ben geïnteresseerd in autotechniek. **d** Ik ben geïnteresseerd in toneel; **3** Some examples: Ik ben niet echt geïnteresseerd in science fiction. Ik ben nogal geïnteresseerd in sport. Ik ben helemaal niet geïnteresseerd in autotechniek. Ik ben vreselijk geïnteresseerd in politiek; **4 c** zaterdag en zondag **d** donderdag **e** dinsdag **f** maandag **g** vrijdag.

Dialogue 3: 1 No, on Friday; **2** Wat zullen we zaterdag doen? Zullen we naar een Chinees restaurant gaan? Ja leuk. O nee, ik kan zaterdag niet. Zondag dan? Ja zondag is ok. Hoe laat zullen we afspreken? Om kwart over twee bij de ingang? Goed. Tot zaterdag dan.

Practice 3: 1 Wat ga je zaterdagmiddag doen? Zaterdagmiddag ga ik nieuwe voetbalschoenen kopen. (Ik ga zaterdagmiddag nieuwe voetbalschoenen kopen.) Wat ga je zondagochtend doen? Zondagochtend ga ik voetballen. (Ik ga zondagochtend voetballen.) **2** Wat gaat Jan zaterdagmiddag doen? Zaterdagmiddag gaat hij nieuwe voetbalschoenen kopen. (Hij gaat zaterdagmiddag nieuwe voetbalschoenen kopen.) Wat gaat Jan zondagmorgen doen? Zondagmorgen gaat hij voetballen. (Hij gaat zondagochtend voetballen.); **3** Wat gaan jullie vrijdagavond doen? Vrijdagavond gaan wij Maria's verjaardag vieren. (Wij gaan vrijdagavond Maria's verjaardag vieren.) Wat gaan jullie zaterdagochtend doen? Zaterdagochtend gaan wij langs de dijk fietsen. (Wij gaan zaterdagochtend langs de dijk fietsen.); **4** Wat gaan Kees en Maria vrijdagavond doen? Vrijdagavond gaan zij Maria's verjaardag vieren. (Zij gaan vrijdagavond Maria's verjaardag vieren.) Wat gaan zij zaterdagochtend doen? Zaterdagochtend gaan ze langs de dijk fietsen. (Zij gaan zaterdagochtend langs de dijk fietsen.); **5** Example sentences: Ik moet les zes herhalen. Ik wil eten koken. Ik ga mijn zoon met zijn huiswerk helpen. Ik wil naar het feest van Maria gaan. Ik moet een cadeau voor Maria kopen. Ik mag foto's in het museum maken.

Unit 8

Discovery question: tweehonderd kilometer

Dialogue 1: spring rolls

Dialogue 2: the steak

Dialogue 3: no, he likes the more expensive t-shirt

Practice: 1 a Waar heeft u zin in? Ik heb zin in een groot feest. Waar heb je zin in? Ik heb zin in een Italiaanse maaltijd. Waar heb je zin in? Ik heb zin in de vakantie. Waar heeft u zin in? Ik heb zin in een lange wandeling. **b** Mevrouw Dijkstal heeft zin in een groot feest. Erwin heeft zin in een Italiaanse maaltijd. Pieter heeft zin in de vakantie. Meneer Paardekoper heeft zin in een lange wandeling; **2 a** aardiger **b** lekkerder, zuurder **c**

lekkerder, zoeter **d** groter, sneller **e** leuker; **3 a** Ik vind dat boek moeilijker. **b** Ik vind die rode broek mooier. **c** Ik vind die krant interessanter. **d** Ik vind dat artikel saaier; **4** Lex is vrolijker dan meneer Heeringa. Meneer Heeringa is verdrietiger/depressiever dan Lex. Lex is optimistischer dan meneer Heeringa. Meneer Heeringa is pessimistischer dan Lex. Lex is jonger dan meneer Heeringa. Meneer Heeringa is ouder dan Lex. Lex is moderner dan meneer Heeringa. Meneer Heeringa is ouderwetser dan Lex. **5** Jane's kleren zijn netter, saaier, ouderwetser, truttiger, hipper, moderner, opvallender, vrouwelijker, fleuriger, goedkoper, duurder, schoner dan die van Els.

Unit 9

Discovery question: U spreekt met (plus your name).

Dialogue 1: 1 five past six; **2** Hallo, met [your name]. Ik sta op Heathrow en neem straks de vlucht van half één. Het vliegtuig komt om half drie in Amsterdam aan. Haal je me dan van het vliegveld op? Bedankt. Tot straks. Dag. **3 a** tot vanmiddag **b** tot zondag **c** tot woensdag **d** tot dinsdag **e** tot volgende week **f** tot volgende maand

Dialogue 2: 1 Frouke van den Broek speaking. **2** She wants to change her appointment. **3** Ja, natuurlijk. **4** Komt morgen je goed uit? **5** No. **6** On Thursday at 10 o'clock. **7** Met (your name). Ik heb een afspraak voor morgen om half twee, maar ik moet dat helaas afzeggen. Kan ik voor een andere keer afspreken? Nee, dat komt mij niet zo goed uit. Woensdag is beter (Kan ik voor woensdag afspreken?) Ja, dat is goed. Dan spreken we woensdag om kwart voor drie af.

Dialogue 3: 1 He's with his mother. **2** Is … thuis?; Kan ik met … spreken?; **3** Kan ik met meneer Plantinga spreken?; **4** Is Menno thuis? **5 a** Met Dirk Jansen. Dag Dirk, met [your name]. Is Alice thuis? Zij is naar een feest, maar zij is morgen (weer) thuis. Goed, ik bel morgen wel. **b** Met de afdeling leningen. Kan ik met mevrouw Blom spreken? Ogenblikje, ik verbind u even door.

Language discovery: a Je reist gemakkelijk en snel van en naar het station. **b** Wat is het tarief voor Het is een (aantrekkelijk) vast tarief per zone. **c** Je boekt NS Zonetaxi (tot 30 minuten van tevoren) via internet of mobiele telefoon. **d** Je betaalt (pas) achteraf via automatische incasso. **e** Je kunt (nog) drie personen meenemen per rit.

Practice: 1 a Ja, we komen morgen mee. **b** Ja, we blijven graag thuis. **c** Ja, ik hang het schilderij in de kamer op. **d** Ja, ik breng de pizza mee. **e** Ja, ik maak het huis schoon; **2 b** Willen Peter en Dries graag thuisblijven? Ja, zij blijven graag thuis. **c** Gaat Lena het schilderij in de kamer ophangen? Ja, zij hangt het in de kamer op. **d** Zal Lena de pizza meebrengen? Ja, zij brengt de pizza mee. **e** Wil Lena het huis schoonmaken? Ja, zij maakt het huis schoon; **3** Dag Harry, met [your name]. Zullen we morgen voetballen? Zullen we zaterdagavond naar de bioscoop (gaan)? Hoe laat zullen we afspreken? Goed, tot zaterdag.

Unit 10

Discovery question: it literally means saving

Language discovery: a Doe straks de boodschappen. **b** Bel me vanavond op. **c** Leer deze les voor morgen. **d** Schrijf oom Jan vanavond. **e** Lees dit artikel. **f** Schreeuw niet zo hard.

Practice: 1 a toch **b** maar **c** toch **d** toch **e** maar **f** toch **g** maar; **2 1** in bottles **2** separate it from normal rubbish **3** a fountain pen **4** don't throw it in the rubbish bin **5** take them to the secondhand shop **6** repair them; **c a** koop **b** scheid **c** gebruik **d** breng **e** breng **f** koop **g** gooi **h** lever … in **i** breng **j** koop, repareer **k** gebruik, neem … mee **l** doe … uit **m** hang … op; **d** Je moet een vulpen in plaats van een wegwerp-pen gebruiken. Je moet je flessen naar de glasbak brengen. Je moet je oud papier naar de papierbak brengen. Je moet tweedehands meubels kopen. Je moet chemisch afval niet in de vuilniszak gooien. Je moet je chemisch afval bij de Chemokar inleveren. Je moet je oude kleren naar de tweedehandswinkel brengen. Je moet niet meteen nieuwe spullen kopen, maar (je moet) kapotte dingen repareren. Je moet geen plastic zakken gebruiken, maar (je moet) je eigen boodschappentas meenemen. Je moet het licht uitdoen (als het niet nodig is). Je moet deze lijst in de keuken ophangen; **3** Bak drie plakjes ham in de koekepan. Doe drie eieren in de pan. Snijd een augurk en tomaat in plakjes. Smeer drie boterhammen. Leg de eieren, de ham, de plakjes tomaat en de augurk boven op de boterham. **4 A** Zet de verwarming lager. **A** Doe de televisie uit als het niet nodig is. **B** Doe de verwarming uit als het niet nodig is. **B** Doe het licht uit als het niet nodig is. **C** Isoleer uw huis. **D** Doe af en toe een raam open. (Note that this instruction can apply to any room in this house!) **E** Neem een douche in plaats van een bad. *Text:* Eén van de makkelijkste manieren om geld te sparen op energie is de verwarming wat lager te zetten. Dus: Zet de verwarming lager. En kamer leeg? De verwarming uit! Dus: Doe de verwarming uit als het niet nodig is. Het is een goed idee uw huis te laten isoleren. Dus: Isoleer uw huis. Maar denkt u eraan, u heeft frisse lucht nodig. Dus: Doe af en toe een raam open. Een bad gebruikt meer water dan een douche. Dus: Neem een douche in plaats van een bad. Dan kunt u ook geld en electriciteit sparen door op de knop te drukken. Dus: Doe het licht uit als het niet nodig is. En: Doe de televisie uit als het niet nodig is..

Grammar summary

In this section you will find a brief explanation of the main grammatical points – and some related information – contained in this book. For more information, look at a grammar book such as *Teach yourself Essential Dutch Grammar*, which is part of this series.

Subject, verb, object

These are three important elements which you will find in many sentences.

SUBJECT

Virtually all sentences have a subject. The subject makes things happen – it is the person, object or idea which performs the action in a sentence. It can be made up of more than one word. Some examples of subjects:

hij	*he*
mijn computer	*my computer*
de nieuwe wereldorde	*the new world order*

VERB

The verb tells you what someone or something is doing. This needn't be anything active. You will find at least one verb in most sentences, but sometimes you will find more than one. Here are some verbs:

eten	*to eat*
dromen	*to dream*
denken	*to think*

OBJECT

This is the person, thing or idea that is at the receiving end of the action in the sentence which is performed by the subject. You won't find an object in all sentences.

Some objects directly undergo the action. These are called direct objects. Other objects 'receive' the direct object. These are called indirect objects. The following sentence contains a <u>direct object</u> and an ***indirect object***:

Hij geeft _zijn telefoonnummer_ **aan** _de vrouw_.

He gives his phone number to the woman.

In this book, we do not make a distinction between direct and indirect objects.

Spelling

a Short vowel sounds are spelt with one vowel in a closed syllable (a syllable ending in a consonant):

man _man_   **hek** _fence/gate_   **bos** _forest_   **bus** _bus_

To keep these syllables closed when adding **-en** (e.g. when a word becomes plural) you double the consonant:

mannen _men_ **hekken** _fences/gates_ **bossen** _forests_ **bussen** _buses_

b Long vowel sounds can be spelt in two ways:

▶ with two vowels in a closed syllable:

maan _moon_   **heer** _gentleman_ **boom** _tree_   **buur** _neighbour_

▶ with one vowel in an open syllable (ending in a vowel):

manen	**heren**	**bomen**	**buren**
moons	_gentlemen_	_trees_	_neighbours_

c A Dutch word cannot end in two consonants if they are the same. This means that a Dutch word never ends in double **l** or **s**, like in English. Compare:

English	_ball_	_bell_
Dutch	**bal**	**bel**

d **z/s** and **v/f**: The letters **z** and **v** are often pronounced as **s** and **f** in Dutch, and at the end of words they are also often written as **s** and **f**. The singular of **brieven** (_letters_), for instance, is **brief** (_letter_) and the singular of **huizen** (_houses_) is **huis** (_house_).

Nouns and articles

ARTICLES

Articles are the words for *the* and *a(n)*. Dutch has three such words: **de** and **het** both mean *the*, and **een** means *a* or *an*. **De** and **het** are the definite articles and **een** is the indefinite article. (See Nouns for when to use **de** and **het**.)

NOUNS

Nouns are words like **auto** (*car*), **thee** (*tea*) and **vakantie** (*holiday, vacation*). Nouns are either countable (things you can count, like **auto** and **vakantie**) or uncountable (things that cannot be counted, like **thee**).

Nouns used without an article or with the indefinite article **een** are called indefinite. You can only use **een** before single countable nouns. Some examples of indefinite nouns:

een lepel	*a spoon*
boeken	*books*

Nouns used with **de** or **het** are called definite nouns. Nouns which have to be combined with **de** are common nouns and nouns which have to be combined with **het** are neuter nouns. Some examples:

de man	*the man*
de vrouw	*the woman*
het kind	*the child*
de badkamer	*the bathroom*
het dorp	*the village*

There are no easy rules to tell you whether a word takes **de** or **het**, so you simply have to learn each one by heart. Note that there are roughly twice as many words with **de** as there are with **het**. All plural nouns take **de**.

singular:	**de vork** (*fork*)	**het mes** (*knife*)
plural:	**de vorken** (*forks*)	**de messen** (*knives*)

COMPOUND NOUNS

Compound nouns are nouns made up of two (or more) other nouns.

In Dutch these are always written as one word:

de telefoon (*telephone*) + **het nummer** (*number*) =
het telefoonnummer

de fles (*bottle*) + **de opener** (*opener*) = **de flesopener**

Compound nouns always take the article from the last part of the word (in **telefoonnummer**, for instance, **het** from **het nummer**).

Sometimes the two nouns are linked by **s**, **e** or **en** to make the new word easier to pronounce:

de stad (*city*) + **het park** (*park*) = **het stadspark**

de erwt (*pea*) + **de soep** (*soup*) = **de erwtensoep**

Plurals

In most cases in Dutch you make a noun plural by adding **-en**:

boek (*book*)	→	**boeken** (*books*)
lamp (*lamp*)	→	**lampen** (*lamps*)

Sometimes the spelling changes when you make a word plural (see the spelling rules in Spelling of the Grammar summary):

huis (*house*)	→	**huizen** (*houses*)
brief (*letter*)	→	**brieven** (*letters*)
pen (*pen*)	→	**pennen** (*pens*)

Some words are made plural by adding **-s**:

computer	→	**computers**
meisje (*girl*)	→	**meisjes** (*girls*)

You will also come across words which are made plural by adding **'s**. These are words ending in **a**, **i**, **o**, **u**, **y** (generally words of foreign, often English, origin):

auto (*car*)	→	**auto's** (*cars*)
euro	→	**euro's**
baby	→	**baby's**

There are also some irregular plural forms:

stad (*city*)	→	**steden** (*cities*)
kind (*child*)	→	**kinderen** (*children*)
ei (*egg*)	→	**eieren** (*eggs*)

Diminutives

Diminutives are words which generally indicate the smallness of something. They usually end in **-je** in Dutch:

het huisje	*little house*
het kopje	*little cup*
het hondje	*little dog*

You will also come across some variations of the **-je** ending, like **-tje**, **-pje**, **-etje**, **-kje**. Note that all diminutives are **het** words.

Diminutives don't just indicate that something is small. Often they add a kind of attitude, to show that you feel something is nice, positive, endearing, not important or sometimes even negative:

een leuk verhaaltje	*a nice story*
mijn ventje	*my lovely little boy*
vreemd zaakje	*strange business, that*

Deze/Die and dit/dat *This and that*

Deze and **dit** are Dutch for *this*, and **die** and **dat** are Dutch for *that*.

Deze and **die** are used in front of **de** words. **Dit** and **dat** are used in front of **het** words.

de hond	*the dog*	**het contract**	*the contract*
deze hond	*this dog*	**dit contract**	*this contract*
die hond	*that dog*	**dat contract**	*that contract*

Since all plural words are de words, you always use **deze** and **die** for plurals:

deze honden	*these dogs*	**deze contracten**	*these contracts*
die honden	*those dogs*	**die contracten**	*those contracts*

Note that **dit** and **dat**, like **het**, can also be used with the verb **zijn** (*to be*) to introduce people or things, both singular or plural. **Deze** and **die** are never used in this way.

dit is mijn mobieltje	*this is my mobile*
dat zijn haar schoenen	*those are her shoes*

Adjectives

Adjectives are words like *blue*, *tall*, *shiny*, *fantastic* and *sweet*, which describe the characteristics of objects, people and ideas.

Sometimes you have to add an extra **-e** to adjectives in Dutch. This happens when the adjective is used directly in front of a noun:

de mooie film   *the beautiful film*

het moderne huis   *the modern house*

However, no **-e** is added when the adjective is used in front of an indefinite **het** word (i.e. a **het** word used with **een** or no article at all):

een modern huis   *a modern house* (**huis** is a **het** word)

Sometimes the spelling of adjectives changes when you add an **-e**:

wit (*white*)   **de witte auto**   *the white car*
groot (*large*)   **een grote boot**   *a big boat*

Comparative and superlative

Comparatives are words like *bigger* and *better*. Superlatives are words such as *biggest* and *best*. To make a comparative, you add **-er** to an adjective. To make a superlative, you add **-st**:

adjective	comparative	superlative
mooi (*beautiful*)	**mooier** (*more beautiful*)	**mooist** (*most beautiful*)
slecht (*bad*)	**slechter** (*worse*)	**slechtst** (*worst*)

The spelling rules apply as usual, of course, and note that with the superlative you always use **het**. In front of a noun, you have to apply the basic rules for adding an **-e** to adjectives.

Haar auto is groter dan mijn auto.   *Her car is bigger than my car.*

Mijn computer is het snelst.   *My computer is the fastest.*

If you are using an adjective ending in an **-r**, you must insert a **d** in the comparative (but not the superlative):

duur	**duurder**	**duurst**
(*expensive*)	(*more expensive*)	(*most expensive*)

Here are some frequently used irregular forms:

goed (*good*)   **beter** (*better*)   **best** (*best*)

veel (*much, many*)   **meer** (*more*)   **meest** (*most*)

weinig (*little, few*)   **minder** (*less, fewer*)   **minst** (*least, fewest*)

Numbers

0–30

0	**nul**				
1	**een, één**	11	**elf**	21	**eenentwintig**
2	**twee**	12	**twaalf**	22	**tweeëntwintig**
3	**drie**	13	**dertien**	23	**drieëntwintig**
4	**vier**	14	**veertien**	24	**vierentwintig**
5	**vijf**	15	**vijftien**	25	**vijfentwintig**
6	**zes**	16	**zestien**	26	**zesentwintig**
7	**zeven**	17	**zeventien**	27	**zevenentwintig**
8	**acht**	18	**achttien**	28	**achtentwintig**
9	**negen**	19	**negentien**	29	**negenentwintig**
10	**tien**	20	**twintig**	30	**dertig**

NB **Een** (*one*) is only written as **één** if it could be confused with the indefinite article **een** (*a/an*). The double dots, or trema, on one of the 'e's in 22, for instance, indicate the start of a new syllable, so you know 22 is pronounced 'twee – en – twintig'.

31–1000.000

31	**eenendertig**	102	**honderdtwee**
32	**tweeëndertig**	115	**honderdvijftien**
40	**veertig**	146	**honderdzesenveertig**
50	**vijftig**	200	**tweehonderd**
60	**zestig**	300	**driehonderd**
70	**zeventig**	789	**zevenhonderdnegenentachtig**
80	**tachtig**	1000	**duizend**
90	**negentig**	100.000	**honderdduizend (een ton)**
100	**honderd**	1000.000	**een miljoen**
101	**honderdeen**		

NB Numbers over 1000 are usually pronounced as units of 100:

1450 = **veertienhonderdvijftig**

For years before 2000, you can leave out **honderd**:

1975 = **negentienhonderdvijfenzeventig** or
negentienvijfenzeventig

FIRST, SECOND, THIRD

Ordinal numbers (numbers like *first*, *second*, *third*) are formed in Dutch by adding **-de** or **-ste** to the numbers. When writing the number in figures, you simply add an **-e**.

1e	**eerste**	11e	**elfde**
2e	**tweede**	12e	**twaalfde**
3e	**derde**	13e	**dertiende**
4e	**vierde**	14e	**veertiende**
5e	**vijfde**	15e	**vijftiende**
6e	**zesde**	16e	**zestiende**
7e	**zevende**	17e	**zeventiende**
8e	**achtste**	18e	**achttiende**
9e	**negende**	19e	**negentiende**
10e	**tiende**	20e	**twintigste**

From 20 most ordinal numbers end in **-ste**. Only those ending with a number under 19 (apart from 1 and 8) end in **-de**.

27e	**zevenentwintigste**
69e	**negenenzestigste**
100e	**honderdste**
116e	**honderdzestiende**
197e	**honderdzevenennegentigste**
1000e	**duizendste**

Weights, measures, time

WEIGHTS

1 gram

1 ons (= 100 gram)

1 pond (= 500 gram)

1 kilo (= 2 pond, 1000 gram)

2 liter

You don't usually use the plural forms of weights, and you don't use the expression of in Dutch:

twee kilo aardappelen	*two kilos of potatoes*
een liter melk	*a litre of milk*

MEASURES

1 mm	**een millimeter**
10 cm	**tien centimeter**
7 m	**zeven meter**
5 m2	**vijf vierkante meter**
50 km	**vijftig kilometer**

You don't usually use the plural forms of these measurements.

TIME

1 minuut	**5 minuten**
1 kwartier (= 15 minuten)	**3 kwartier**
1 uur	**2 uur**
1 week	**3 weken**
1 maand	**6 maanden**
1 jaar	**10 jaar**

There are plural forms of **kwartier**, **uur** and **jaar** (they are **kwartieren**, **uren** and **jaren**), but you don't usually use them.

Personal pronouns

Personal pronouns are words like *I*, *you*, *he* and *me*, *her*, *us*, etc. Personal pronouns are divided into subject pronouns and object pronouns.

Subject pronouns are used as the subject of the sentence, i.e. the person(s) to whom the subject pronoun refers is/are performing the action. The verb changes its form depending on the subject pronoun which you're using:

ik fiets	*I'm cycling*	**wij fietsen**	*we are cycling*

Object pronouns function as the object in the sentence, i.e. the person(s) to whom it refers is/are not performing the action expressed by the verb:

ik hou van hem   *I love him*   **zij houdt van mij**   *she loves me*

	Subject pronouns			Object pronouns		
	stressed	unstressed		stressed	unstressed	
singular	ik	('k)	*I*	**mij**	**me**	*me*
	jij	je	*you (informal)*	**jou**	**je**	*you (informal)*
	u	—	*you (formal)*	**u**	—	*you (formal)*
	hij	(ie)	*he*	**hem**	('m)	*him*
	zij	ze	*she*	**haar**	(d'r)	*her*
	het	('t)	*it*	**het**	('t)	*it*
plural	wij	**we**	*we*	**ons**	—	*us*
	jullie	—	*you (informal)*	**jullie**	—	*you (informal)*
	u	—	*you (formal)*	**u**	—	*you (formal)*
	zij	ze	*they*	**hen/ hun***	**ze**	*them*

The unstressed forms in brackets are not generally used in writing.

*The rules for when to use **hen** or **hun** are quite tricky (**hen** is used as a direct object and after prepositions) and consequently many Dutch people often make mistakes with this and use **hen** and **hun** interchangeably. Luckily, **ze** is correct in nearly all cases, so if you stick to **ze** you (almost) never will be wrong.

NB When speaking, generally the unstressed forms of the pronouns are used, except when you want to stress the pronoun or emphasize a contrast:

Ik werk maar hij niet.   *I work but he doesn't.*

FORMAL/INFORMAL

The informal pronouns are used when speaking to people with whom you are on a first-name basis, e.g. children, young people, relatives, friends, acquaintances, colleagues. The formal pronoun **u** is used when addressing people with whom you are not on a first-name basis, e.g. people you don't know, like shop assistants (unless very young), and people to whom you wish to show respect or social distance, such as your boss.

REFERRING TO THINGS

When referring to things, you use **het** if you are referring to a **het** word and **hij** or **hem** when referring to a **de** word. For plurals you use **ze**.

Waar is het boek?	*Where is the book?*
Kijk, daar is het.	*Look there it is.*
Is de film goed?	*Is it a good film?*
Ja, hij is fantastisch.	*Yes, it is fantastic.*
Heb jij de sleutels?	*Do you have the keys?*
Nee, ik heb ze niet.	*No, I don't have them.*

	subject pronoun	object pronoun
het word:	**het**	**het**
de word:	**hij**	**hem**
plural word:	**ze**	**ze**

Possession

POSSESSIVE PRONOUNS

Possessive pronouns indicate who is the owner of something and work in the same way in Dutch as they do in English: *my, your, his,* etc.

	stressed	unstressed	
singular	**mijn**	**(m'n)**	*my*
	jouw	**je**	*your* (informal)
	uw	**–**	*your* (formal)
	zijn	**(z'n)**	*his*
	haar	**(d'r)**	*her*
plural	**ons/onze***	**–**	*our*
	jullie	**je**	*your* (informal)
	uw	**–**	*your* (formal)
	hun	**–**	*their*

The unstressed forms in brackets are not generally used in writing.

* **ons** is used before **het** words and **onze** is used before de words:

ons woordenboek	*our dictionary*
onze tuin	*our garden*

VAN ... OF

Possession can also be expressed in Dutch by using an **-s**, like in English:

Johans hond *Johan's dog*

Linda's kat *Linda's cat*

(An apostrophe is only used if the **-s** would change the pronunciation of the sound preceding it.)

However, it is much more usual in Dutch to use **van**:

Is dit de hond van Johan?	*Is this Johan's dog?*
Heb jij dat boek van mijn moeder?	*Do you have that book of my mother's?*

Verbs

WHAT ARE VERBS?

Verbs are 'doing' words which often describe an activity or an action like **lopen** (*to walk*), **denken** (*to think*), **lachen** (*to laugh*).

THE INFINITIVE

The basic form of the verb is the infinitive and in Dutch usually ends in **-en** (in English, this is the form of the verb with *to*: **dromen** *to dream*).

THE STEM

You will have seen that verbs change their form. Most of the forms a verb can take are based on the stem of the verb. The stem of the verb is the form that goes with **ik**, which you can find by taking the **-en** ending off the infinitive:

infinitive:	**werken** (*to work*)	**kopen** (*to buy*)	**rennen** (*to run*)
stem:	**werk**	**koop**	**ren**

Note that the spelling rules apply when you take away **-en**.

WHICH FORM?

Which form of the verb you need to use depends on the subject of the sentence. For **hij** (*he*) and **zij** (*she*), for instance, you add a **-t** to the stem, and for **wij** (*we*), you use the infinitive form of the verb.

WORD ORDER

You will generally find the (first) verb in a Dutch sentence in second position (i.e. the second 'item' in a sentence, not necessarily the second word), although sometimes you will find a verb at the very beginning of questions.

Ik kook bijna nooit. — *I almost never cook.*

Gwynneth en Peter zijn te laat. — *Gwynneth and Peter are late.*

Gaan zij ook op vakantie? — *Are they also going on holiday?*

The present tense

FORM: REGULAR VERBS

For the present tense forms of regular Dutch verbs, you add either **-t** or **-en** to the stem of the verb. This is best illustrated with an example like **werken** (*to work*):

ik	**werk**	**we/wij**	**werken**
je/jij	**werkt**	**jullie**	**werken**
u	**werkt**	**u**	**werkt**
hij/zij/het	**werkt**	**ze/zij**	**werken**

INVERSION

Sometimes the subject has to be placed after the verb. This is called inversion. It happens, for instance, when you're asking a question:

Heb jij die CD ook? — *Do you have that CD as well?*

When this happens with **je** or **jij**, i.e. when **je** or **jij** appear after the verb, then the **-t** is dropped from the verb. This only happens with **je** and **jij**, but applies to all verbs.

Jij werkt hard. *You are working hard.*

Werk jij hard? *Are you working hard?*

USE

In Dutch the present tense can be used to talk about something which is happening here and now:

Ik lees een boek. *I'm reading a book.*

However, often the present tense is also used to talk about the future:

Ik ga morgen naar New York. *I'm going to New York tomorrow.*

You can also use the present tense to talk about things which started in the past and continue in the present. However, in this case you must use **al**, **pas** or **nu**:

Ik kom hier al tien jaar. *I've been coming here for (as long as) ten years.*

Zij werkt hier pas een maand. *She's only been working here for a month.*

Wij wonen hier nu een jaar. *We've been living here for a year now.*

With **al** you indicate that you think something has been a long time and with **pas** that you think it's only been a short time.

Modal verbs

Some verbs don't actually describe an action or activity but are used in combination with other verbs for a different purpose. An important group of such verbs are the modal verbs. Modal verbs express various meanings such as saying what you *can*, *wish*, *may*, *must* or *should*.

WORD ORDER

Modal verbs are combined with another verb. This second verb always comes at the end of the sentence and is always in the infinitive form:

Zij wil een CD kopen. *She wants to buy a CD.*

Ben moet de was doen. *Ben has to do the washing.*

When used with the modal verb **hoeven** the infinitive at the end is always preceded by **te**:

Ben hoeft de was niet te doen. *Ben doesn't have to do the washing.*

If the infinitive at the end of the sentence is hebben or gaan, it is often left out:

Wij willen een biertje (hebben). *We want (to have) a beer.*

Ik moet naar het station (gaan). *I have (to go) to the railway station.*

FORM

The forms of the modal verbs are irregular.

	zullen	willen	kunnen	mogen	moeten	hoeven**
	will	*want*	*can/be able to*	*may/be allowed*	*must/have to*	*(don't) have to*
ik	zal	wil	kan	mag	moet	hoef
jij	zal/zult*	wil/wilt*	kan/kunt*	mag	moet	hoeft
u	zal/zult*	wil/wilt*	kan/kunt*	mag	moet	hoeft
hij/zij/het	zal	wil	kan	mag	moet	hoeft
wij	zullen	willen	kunnen	mogen	moeten	hoeven
jullie	zullen	willen	kunnen	mogen	moeten	hoeven
u	zal/zult*	wil/wilt*	kan/kunt*	mag	moet	hoeft
zij	zullen	willen	kunnen	mogen	moeten	hoeven

* **Zult**, **wilt** and **kunt** are more formal than **zal**, **wil** and **kan**.

** **Hoeven** is only used in negative contexts, i.e. when you don't have to do something.

Separable verbs

Separable verbs are made up of two parts which are sometimes separated when used in a sentence. The two parts are the prefix and the main part of the verb. For instance, **uit** (*out*) and **gaan** (*to go*) together make up the separable verb **uitgaan** (*to go out*). Some other separable verbs are:

weggaan	*to go away*	**opeten**	*to eat up*
opbellen	*to call up*	**uitgeven**	*to spend*
aankomen	*to arrive*	**ophangen**	*to hang up*

WHEN TO SEPARATE?

When used in a sentence, the main part of the separable verb takes its ordinary place as the main verb at the beginning of the sentence. The prefix is moved to the very end.

Ik hang mijn kleren op.   *I'm hanging up my clothes.*

Geef jij altijd zoveel geld uit?   *Do you always spend this much money?*

WHEN NOT TO SEPARATE?

When a separable verb is used with another verb, e.g. a modal verb, then the whole verb appears at the end of the sentence.

Wil jij het restaurant opbellen?	*Do you want to call the restaurant?*
Jantje moet alles opeten!	*Jantje has to eat up everything!*

If you combine a verb with **hoeven** (*not have to*), then you need to put **te** in front of the infinitive at the end of the sentence. If this infinitive is a separable verb, **te** splits up the two parts of the separable verb:

Je hoeft niet alles op te eten.	*You don't have to eat up everything.*

Imperative

The imperative is a verb form which is used to give commands and instructions, for example *come!, sit down!* and *leave!* In Dutch, the imperative is made with the stem of the verb.

Kom hier.	*Come here.*

With separable verbs the prefix comes last.

Ga weg.	*Go away.*
Kom binnen.	*Come in.*

Note that Dutch also often uses the infinitive form of verbs to give instructions. For example:

Niet parkeren.	*No parking.* (lit. *not to park*)

Talking about the future

There are three different ways of talking about the future in Dutch.

THE PRESENT TENSE

Simply using the present tense is the most common way of talking about the future.

Ik ben er vanavond niet.	*I won't be there tonight.*
We kopen morgen een zeilboot.	*We'll buy a sailing boat tomorrow.*

GAAN *TO GO*

Combining a form of the verb **gaan** (*to go*) with an infinitive at the end of the sentence is another common way of talking about the future.

| **Marion gaat morgen winkelen.** | *Marion's going shopping tomorrow.* |
| **Wanneer gaan jullie tennissen?** | *When are you going to play tennis?* |

ZULLEN *WILL*

Zullen is the verb with which to form the future tense proper: **zullen** + an infinitive at the end of the sentence. However, **zullen** isn't used as often as the present tense or **gaan** to refer to the future. The main reason for using **zullen** is to make a promise or to give a guarantee.

Ik zal het proberen. *I will try.*

Mijn collega zal het voor u regelen. *My colleague will arrange it for you.*

Negatives

Sentences can be made negative in Dutch by using either **niet** or **geen**. There is no need to add a verb like *to do*, as you often have to in English.

NIET *NOT*

Niet simply means *not* and is the most common way of making sentences negative. **Niet** is generally placed at the very end of a sentence:

| **Ik begrijp het niet.** | *I don't understand (it).* |

There are a few exceptions to this rule. **Niet** is always put in front of:

1 verbs which are placed at the end (see under modal verbs, for instance)

| **Hij wil zijn huiswerk niet doen.** | *He doesn't want to do his homework.* |

2 prepositions (words like *in, on, under, with,* **etc.)**

| **We gaan niet naar de bioscoop.** | *We're not going to the cinema.* |

3 descriptive words like adjectives

| **Vind jij Rembrandt niet mooi?** | *You don't find Rembrandt beautiful?* |

GEEN *NOT ONE/NOT ANY*

Geen is used in combination with indefinite nouns (nouns which are used with **een** or without an article at all).

Heb jij een pen?	*Do you have a pen?*
Nee, ik heb geen pen.	*No, I don't have a pen.*
Wil je melk?	*Would you like milk?*

Nee, ik wil geen melk.	*No, I don't want any milk.*
Heb jij postzegels?	*Do you have any stamps?*
Nee, ik heb geen postzegels.	*No, I don't have any stamps.*

OTHER NEGATIVES

Here are some other useful words or ways of expressing something negative.

▶ **nog niet/nog geen** (*not yet*): when something hasn't happened yet:

We zijn nog niet klaar.	*We're not ready yet.*
Ik heb nog geen DVD-speler.	*I don't have a DVD player yet.*

▶ **niet meer/geen … meer** (*not any more*): when something has ended:

Ze heeft die auto niet meer.	*She doesn't have that car any more.*
Ik wil geen wijn meer.	*I don't want any more wine.*

▶ **nergens** (*nowhere*), **nooit** (*never*), **niemand** (*no one*), **niets** (*nothing*).

Ik kan nooit mijn sleutels vinden.	*I can never find my keys.*

Time, manner, place

When talking about the time when something takes place, the manner (or with whom) and the location of what you're describing in Dutch, then this information is usually given in exactly this order: time – manner – place.

Peter gaat morgen (time) **met de auto** (manner)
naar Amsterdam (place).

Peter is going to Amsterdam by car tomorrow.

As you can see, the standard order in English is place – manner – time. As in English, this order isn't absolute and it can be changed to highlight certain information, for instance, or to stress a particular point.

Hij gaat naar Groningen morgen!	*He's going to Groningen tomorrow!*

Prepositions

Here are some frequently used prepositions. Note that the meaning of prepositions often depends on the context, so may not always be as straightforward as this list suggests.

in	*in*	**op**	*on*
onder	*under*	**voor**	*in front of, for*
achter	*behind*	**naast**	*next to*
over	*over*	**tussen**	*between*
tegen	*against*	**uit**	*from, out of*
bij	*at, near*	**door**	*through, by*
naar	*to*	**na**	*after*

Dutch–English vocabulary

aan	*on, to*
aangeven	*to indicate*
(zich) aankleden	*to get dressed*
aankomen	*to arrive*
aantrekkelijk	*attractive*
de aardappel	*potato*
de aardbei	*strawberry*
aardig	*nice*
de abrikoos	*apricot*
de acteur	*actor*
actief	*active*
de activiteit	*activity*
de actrice	*actress*
de administrateur	*administrator*
adoreren	*to adore*
het adres	*address*
het advies	*advice*
de advocaat	*lawyer*
de afdeling	*department*
afgesproken	*agreed*
afhalen	*to collect*
afmaken	*to finish*
de afrit, de afslag	*(motorway) exit*
afronden	*to round off*
de afspraak	*appointment, arrangement*
afspreken	*to make an appointment, arrange*

het afval	*rubbish*
afzeggen	*to cancel (an appointment)*
al	*already*
al met al	*all in all*
allebei	*both*
alledaags	*everyday-like*
alleen	*only, alone*
allemaal	*all*
allerlei	*all sorts of*
altijd	*always*
(zich) amuseren	*to amuse oneself*
analyseren	*to analyse*
de ananas	*pineapple*
ander	*other*
anderhalf	*one and a half*
anders	*otherwise*
de andijvie	*endive*
de apotheek	*pharmacist*
de appel	*apple*
de arm	*arm*
het artikel	*article*
artistiek	*artistic*
de aspirine	*aspirin*
de assistent(e)	*assistant*
de augurk	*gherkin*
de automaat	*machine*
de autosnelweg	*motorway*
de avond	*evening*
de baan	*job*
bakken	*to fry*
de bakker	*baker*
de bal	*ball*

de banaan	*banana*
de bank	*bank*
de bankassistent(e)	*bank employee*
bazig	*bossy*
bedankt	*thanks*
bedoelen	*to mean*
het bedrijf	*company*
de bedrijfscultuur	*company culture*
het been	*leg*
een beetje	*a little*
beginnen	*to begin*
begrijpen	*to understand*
behalve	*except*
bekritiseren	*to criticize*
belangrijk	*important*
belegen	*mature (cheese)*
de belegen kaas	*mature cheese*
bellen	*to ring*
bepaald	*certain*
beperken	*limit/restrict*
bereid	*prepared*
de berg	*mountain*
het beroep	*profession*
beslist	*certainly*
besluiteloos	*indecisive*
bestaan	*to exist*
bestellen	*to order*
betalen	*to pay*
de betaling	*payment*
betekenen	*to mean*
beter	*better*
betrouwbaar	*reliable*

de beurt	turn
bewolkt	cloudy
bezitten	to possess
het bezoek	visit
de bibliothecaris (-esse)	librarian
bieden	to offer
de biefstuk	steak
het bier	beer
bij	at, by, in, near
bijna	nearly
het biljet	note (money)
binnen	inside
de bioscoop	cinema
blauw	blue
blijven	to stay
de bloem	flower
de bloemkool	cauliflower
boeiend	exciting
het boek	book
boeken	to book
de boer (in)	farmer
het bolletje	roll (bread)
boodschappen	shopping
Boogschutter	Sagittarius
de boon	bean
borduren	to embroider
de borrel	strong drink
het bos	wood
de boter	butter
de boterham	sandwich
boven	above
breien	to knit

brengen	*to bring*
de briefkaart	postcard
de bril	*glasses*
de broek	*trousers*
de broer	*brother*
het broodje	*(bread) roll*
bruin	*brown*
de bui	*shower (of rain)*
de buik	*stomach*
buiten	*outside*
buitenland	*abroad*
de bushalte	*bus stop*
de buurt	*neighbourhood*
het cadeau	*gift*
camoufleren	*to disguise/camouflage*
de camping	*campsite*
het centrum	*centre*
chagrijnig	*moody*
de chauffeur	*driver*
de chocola	*chocolate*
het colbert	*jacket*
comfortabel	*comfortable*
daar	*there*
daarna	*next*
daarnaast	*next to*
de dag	*day*
dan	*then*
danken	*to thank*
dansen	*to dance*
dat	*that*
delen	*to share*
denken	*to think*

de deur	*door*
deze	*this, these*
dicht	*shut*
de dienst	*service*
de dijk	*dyke*
dik	*fat*
dineren	*to dine*
het ding	*thing*
dit	*this*
de docent(e)	*lecturer*
de dochter	*daughter*
doen	*to do*
de dokter	*doctor*
dol	*mad*
dom	*stupid*
domineren	*to dominate*
donker	*dark*
doorverbinden	*to connect*
het dorp	*village*
dorst hebben	*to be thirsty*
dragen	*to wear, carry*
de drank	*drink*
dringend	*urgent*
drinken	*to drink*
de drogist	*chemist*
droog	*dry*
de drop	*liquorice*
de druif	*grape*
druk	*busy*
drukken	*to press, print*
duidelijk	*obvious*
duizeligheid	*dizziness*

dun	*thin*
dus	*so, thus*
duur	*expensive*
echt	*real, really*
effen	*plain*
egoïstisch	*selfish*
het ei (pl. eieren)	*egg*
eigen	*own*
eigenlijk	*really, actually*
het eind	*end*
de electriciteit	*electricity*
het elftal	*team (of eleven)*
elk	*each*
elkaar	*each other*
emailen	*to send an email*
de energie	*energy*
energiek	*energetic*
de enige	*the only one*
enkel	*single*
er	*there*
ergens	*somewhere*
eruitzien	*to look (like)*
de ervaring	*experience*
de erwt	*pea*
eten	*to eat*
etenswaren	*food*
de euro (pl. euro's)	*euro*
evenveel	*as much*
de familie	*family*
het familieleven	*family life*
fanatiek	*fanatical*
fantastisch	*fantastic*

favoriet	*favourite*
het feest	*party*
de fiets	*bicycle*
fietsen	*to cycle*
de file	*traffic jam*
filosofisch	*philosophical*
de fles	*bottle*
de foto	*photograph*
fraai	*pretty*
de framboos	*raspberry*
gaan	*to go*
gaan met …	*to go out with …*
de garnaal	*prawn*
gebaseerd op	*based on*
geboekt	*booked*
geboren	*born*
het gebrek aan	*(the) lack of*
gebroken	*broken*
gebruiken	*to use*
gedisciplineerd	*disciplined*
geduldig	*patient*
geel	*yellow*
geen	*no*
het gehakt	*mince*
de geitenkaas	*goat's cheese*
gek zijn op	*to be crazy about*
geldig	*valid*
gelijk	*equal*
de gemeente	*municipality*
het geneesmiddel	*medicine*
genieten	*to enjoy*
de geschiedenis	*history*

het gesprek	*conversation*
gestreept	*striped*
gevaarlijk	*dangerous*
geven	*to give*
het gevoel	*sense/feeling*
gevoelig	*sensitive*
het gevolg	*result*
gevuld	*filled*
geweldig	*terrific*
het gewicht	*weight*
gewoon	*ordinary, just*
gezellig	*cosy, fun to be around*
het gezin	*family*
gezond	*healthy*
de gids	*guide*
het glas	*glass*
glimlachen	*to smile*
goed	*good*
goedaardig	*good-hearted*
goedkoop	*cheap*
gooien	*to throw*
graag	*please*
de gracht	*canal (in towns)*
de griep	*flu*
de griezelfilm	*horror film*
grijs	*grey*
groen	*green*
de groente	*vegetable*
de groenteboer	*greengrocer*
groot	*big*
de grootouder	*grandparent*
het haar	*hair*

de haast	*haste*
haasten	*to hurry*
de hagelslag	*hundreds and thousands*
halen	*to fetch*
de halfvolle melk	*semi-skimmed milk*
de hals	*neck*
het hapje	*snack*
hard	*fast*
hartelijk	*warm, affectionate*
hebben	*to have*
heel	*very, whole*
heel veel	*a great many things*
heerlijk	*lovely*
heidevelden	*moors*
helaas	*unfortunately*
helpen	*to help*
de herfst	*autumn*
herhalen	*to repeat*
heten	*to be called*
hier	*here*
hoe	*how*
de hoek	*corner*
de hoest	*cough*
hoesten	*to cough*
hoeveel	*how much*
honger hebben	*to be hungry*
het hoofd	*head*
de hoofdstad	*capital*
het hoofdgerecht	*main course*
de hooikoorts	*hay fever*
houden van	*to like*
het huis	*house*

de huisarts	*general practitioner*
huiselijk	*homely*
het huisje	*cottage/cabin*
het huiswerk	*homework*
humeurig	*cross, moody*
humor	*humour*
het idee	*idea*
ieder	*each*
iemand	someone
iets	*something*
het ijs	*ice, ice cream*
ijverig	*industrious*
de ingang	*entrance*
ingewikkeld	*complicated*
inleveren	*to hand in*
de innerlijke	*rust inner peace*
instappen	*to get in*
integer	*honest/honourable*
interessant	*interesting*
(zich) interesseren	*to be interested*
de invloed	*influence*
irriteren	*to irritate*
het jaar	*year*
het jaargetijde	*season*
jaloers	*jealous*
jarig, ik ben~	*it's my birthday*
de jas	*jacket*
jeuken	*to itch*
jong	*young*
de jonge kaas	*young cheese*
de jongen	*boy*
de jurk	*dress*

de jus d'orange	orange juice
de kaart	map, ticket
het kaartje	ticket
de kaas	cheese
de kabeljauw	cod
de kam	comb
de kamer	room
kamperen	to camp
de kans	chance
het kantoor	office
kapot	broken
de kapsalon	hairdressers
de karaktereigenschap	(personal) characteristic
de karaktertrek	(personal) characteristic
de kassa	checkout
de keel	throat
de keer	turn, time
de kennis	acquaintance, knowledge
de kerk	church
de ketting	necklace
de keuken	kitchen
de keuze	choice
kijken	to look
het kind (pl. kinderen)	child
de kip	chicken
klaar staan	to be ready
de klant	client, customer
klein	small
het kleingeld	change
kleinzielig	small-minded
klemmen	to stick, jam
de kleren (pl.)	clothes

kletsen	*to chat*
de kleur	*colour*
knap	*good-looking (also clever)*
knippen	*to cut (with scissors)*
de knop	*handle*
de koekepan	*frying pan*
het koekje	*biscuit*
koel	*cool, cold*
de koffer	*suitcase*
de koffie	*coffee*
koken	*to cook*
komen	*to come*
het kompas	*compass*
de kool	*cabbage*
de koorts	*fever*
kopen	*to buy*
koppig	*headstrong*
kort	*short*
kosten	*to cost*
koud	*cold*
de kracht	*strength*
de krant	*newspaper*
de krat	*crate*
de kreeft	*lobster*
Kreeft	*Cancer*
krijgen	*to get*
de kroeg	*bar/café/pub*
de kruidenier	*grocer*
het kruispunt	*crossroads*
de krul	*curl*
het kuipje	*tub*
kunnen	*to be able*

de kunst	*art*
de kunstenaar (-ares)	*artist*
kussen	*to kiss*
het kwart	*quarter*
de kwestie	*matter*
kwetsbaar	*vulnerable*
de kwetsbaarheid	*vulnerability*
de laars	*boot*
laat	*late*
het lamsvlees	*lamb (meat)*
het land	*country*
lang	*long*
langs	*along*
langzaam	*slow, slowly*
laten	*to allow, let*
de leeftijd	*age*
leeg	*empty*
Leeuw	*Leo*
leggen	*to put, lay*
de leider	*leader*
lekker	*tasty*
lenen	*to lend, borrow*
de lening	*loan*
de lente	*spring*
de leraar (-ares)	*teacher*
leren	*to teach, learn*
de les	*lesson*
letten op	*to pay attention to*
leuk	*nice*
lezen	*to read*
het lichaam	*body*
het licht	*light*

licht	*light*
liefhebbend	*loving*
liever	*rather*
de lijn	*route, line*
de lijst	*list*
links	*(to the) left*
de literatuur	*literature*
de loempia	*spring roll*
logeren	*to stay*
het loket	*ticket office*
de lokettist(e)	*ticket clerk*
loom	*sluggish*
lopen	*to walk*
de lucht	*air*
luisteren	*to listen*
lunchen	*to have lunch*
de lunchpauze	*lunch break*
de maag	*stomach*
Maagd	*Virgo*
de maaltijd	*meal*
de maand	*month*
maar	*but*
de maat	*size*
mager	*thin*
de magere melk	*skimmed milk*
magnifiek	*magnificent*
maken	*to make*
makkelijk	*easy*
de manier	*manner, way*
de martelaar	*martyr*
matig	*moderate*
de medestudent	*fellow student*

de medewerker (-ster)	assistant
meebrengen	to bring with you
meekomen	to come with
meenemen	to take with
het meer	lake
meer	more
meest	most
meestal	usually
het meisje	girl
de melk	milk
de meloen	melon
de mening	opinion
de mens	person
meteen	straightaway
het meubel	piece of furniture
het midden	middle
minder	less
minst	least
de minuut	minute
misschien	perhaps
misselijk	sick
het mobieltje	mobile phone
de mode	fashion
modieus	fashionable
moe	tired
de moeder	mother
moederlijk	motherly
moeilijk	difficult
moeten	to have to
mogen	to be permitted to
de mond	mouth
mooi	beautiful

de morgen	*morning*
morgen	*tomorrow*
de mossel	*mussel*
de motor	*motorbike*
de mouw	*sleeve*
de munt	*coin*
de muziek	*music*
na	*after*
de naam	*name*
naar	*to*
naast	*next*
de nacht	*night*
nadenken	*to think about*
het nagerecht	*dessert*
het najaar	*autumn*
nat	*wet*
de nationaliteit	*nationality*
het natuurgebied	*nature area*
natuurlijk	*natural, naturally*
de neiging	*tendency*
nemen	*to take*
net	*neat*
het netwerk	*network*
niets	*nothing*
nieuw	*new*
nodig	*necessary*
nog	*yet, still*
nogal	*quite*
nu	*now*
het nummer	*number*
de ober	*waiter*
de ochtend	*morning*

de oefening	*exercise*
het ogenblikje	*moment*
de olie	*oil*
om	*about, around*
de oma	grandma
omgaan	*to go round (with)*
de omgeving	*surroundings*
ondankbaar	*ungrateful*
het ontbijt	*breakfast*
ontbijten	*to have breakfast*
ontdekken	*to discover*
ontmoeten	*to meet*
ontspannen	*to relax*
de onweersbui	*thunderstorm*
onweerstaanbaar	*irresistible*
onweren	*to storm*
onzorgvuldig	*careless/sloppy*
het oog	*eye*
ook	*also*
de oom	*uncle*
het oor	*ear*
de opa	*grandpa*
opbellen	*to ring up*
openbaar	*public*
ophalen	*to fetch*
ophangen	*to hang up*
oplossen	*to solve*
opnemen	*to pick up*
oppassen	*to look after, to be careful, to babysit*
opschrijven	*to write down*
opstaan	*to get up*

opzoeken	*to visit*
oranje	*orange (colour)*
organiseren	*to organize*
oud	*old*
de oude kaas	*extra mature cheese*
de ouder	*parent*
ouderwets	*old-fashioned*
overal	*everywhere*
overdekt	*covered*
overheerlijk	*delicious*
het overhemd	*shirt*
overstappen	*to change (buses, etc.)*
oversteken	*to cross (road)*
het overwerk	*overtime*
het paar	*pair*
een paar	*few*
paars	*purple*
het pak	*suit/carton*
het pakje	*parcel*
pakken	*to pack/fetch*
het papier	*paper*
pas	*not until*
passen	*to try on*
passeren	*to pass*
de patat	*chips (French fries)*
de pauze	*break*
de peer	*pear*
het perron	*platform*
de persoon	*person*
de perzik	*peach*
het petje	*cap*
de pijn	*pain*

het pilletje	*pill*
de pils	*beer*
het pilsje	*glass of beer*
de pindakaas	*peanut butter*
pinnen	*to pay by card/get money from a cashpoint*
de pincode	*pin code*
de plaats	*place*
plaatselijk	*local*
het plakje	*slice*
het plastic tasje	*plastic bag*
het platteland	*country(side)*
de poes	*cat*
de politie	*police*
de politieagent	*policeman/woman*
het politiebureau	*police station*
het postkantoor	*post office*
de pot	*jar*
prachtig	*wonderful*
de praktijk	*practice (doctor's)*
praktisch	*practical*
praten	*to talk*
de prei	*leek*
pretentieus	*pretentious*
het pretpark	*theme park*
prettig	*nice*
de prioriteit	*priority*
privé	*private*
het probleem	*problem*
het programma	*programme*
het project	*project*
punctueel	*punctual*

het puntje	crusty roll
het raam	window
raar	strange
de radijs	radish
Ram	Aries
reageren op	to react to
het recept	recipe, prescription
rechtdoor	straight ahead
rechts	(to the) right
redelijk	reasonable
de redacteur	editor
de reden	reason
de regen	rain
de reis	journey
reizen	to travel
het reisbureau	travel agent
de rekening	account
de relatie	relationship
repareren	to repair
de restauratie	station buffet
het retour	return
riant	ample/considerable
de richting	direction
de riem	belt
rijden	to drive
de rijst	rice
het risico	risk
de rok	skirt
romantisch	romantic
rond	round
rood	red
de room	cream

de rotonde	*roundabout*
de rug	*back*
de rugzak	*rucksack*
het rundvlees	*beef*
rustig	*quiet*
saai	*boring*
samen	*together*
het sap	*juice*
schaatsen	*to skate*
schaken	*to play chess*
de schelvis	*haddock*
schijnen	*to seem*
schilderen	*to paint*
het schilderij	*painting*
schitterend	*marvellous, wonderful*
de schoen	*shoe*
de schol	*plaice*
schoonmaken	*to clean*
Schorpioen	*Scorpio*
de schotel	*dish, meal*
de schouwburg	*theatre*
schreeuwen	*to scream*
schrijven	*to write*
de secretaresse	*secretary*
de sinaasappel	*orange (fruit)*
de sinaasappelsap	*orange juice*
sinds	*since*
skeeleren	*in-line skating*
de sla	*lettuce*
de slaapzak	*sleeping bag*
de slager	*butcher*
slank	*slim*

slapen	*to sleep*
slecht	*bad*
slechts	*only*
de sleutel	*key*
slim	*smart/clever*
de sluis	*lock (canal, etc.)*
smaken	*to taste*
smeren	*to spread*
sneeuwen	*to snow*
snel	*fast*
snijden	*to cut*
het snoepje	*sweet*
sociaal	*socially minded*
de soep	*soup*
soms	*sometimes*
het soort	*type*
het souterrain	*basement*
spa blauw	*still mineral water*
spa rood	*sparkling mineral water*
sparen	*to save*
de speelfilm	*film*
spelen	*to play*
de sperzieboon	*green bean*
de spijkerbroek	*jeans*
de spinazie	*spinach*
spiritueel	spiritualhet
spoorboekje	*railway timetable*
de spoorweg	*railway*
sporten	*to play sport*
het spreekuur	*surgery time*
spreken	*to speak*
staan	*to stand*

de stad (pl. steden)	*town*
star	*uncompromising*
het statiegeld	*extra charge on glass bottles*
Steenbok	*Capricorn*
stempelen	*to cancel (ticket)*
sterk	*strong*
Stier	*Taurus*
stijf	*stiff*
stil	*quiet*
de stoel	*chair*
het stoplicht	*traffic light*
stoppen	*to stop*
storen	*to disturb*
de straat	*street*
strak	*tight*
straks	*soon*
de strip	*comic*
de stropdas	*(neck) tie*
studeren	*to study*
de studie	*studies*
het stuk	*piece*
de suiker	*sugar*
de supermarkt	*supermarket*
sympathiek	*sympathetic*
het symptoom	*symptom*
het systeem	*system*
de taal	*language*
tactvol	*tactful*
de tafel	*table*
tamelijk	*fairly*
de tandarts	*dentist*
de tandenborstel	*toothbrush*

de tandpasta	*toothpaste*
de tante	*aunt*
de tas	*bag*
tegen	*against, to*
de tekst	*text*
de telefoon	*telephone*
het telefoonnummer	*telephone number*
tennissen	*to play tennis*
de tentoönstelling	*exhibition*
het terras	*outdoor patio of a restaurant/terrace*
terug	*back*
terugkomen	*to come back*
de thee	*tea*
thuis	*at home*
de tijd	*time*
het tijdschrift	*magazine*
toch	*nevertheless*
de tocht	*trip*
het toetje	*'afters', dessert*
de tomaat	*tomato*
het toneel	*stage*
tot	*to*
traag	*slow*
de trap	*stairs*
de trein	*train*
de trekkershut	*cabin*
trouwens	*indeed*
de trui	*sweater*
de tuin	*garden*
tussen	*between*
tweedehands	*secondhand*

Tweelingen	*Gemini*
de ui	*onion*
uit	*out*
de uitdaging	*challenge*
uitgebreid	*extensive, elaborate*
uitgeven	*to spend*
uitkleden	*to undress*
uitlaten	*to walk (a dog)*
uitreiken	*to give out*
de uitslag	*result*
het uitstapje	*trip*
uitstekend	*excellent*
het uitzicht	*view*
de universiteit	*university*
het uur	*hour*
vaak	*often*
de vader	*father*
de vakantie	*holiday*
vallen	*to fall*
van	*of, from*
vanaf	*from*
vanavond	*this evening*
vandaag	*today*
vanmiddag	*this afternoon*
vanochtend	*this morning*
vanuit	*from*
varen	to sailhet
varkensvlees	*pork*
veel	*much, many*
veeleisend	*demanding*
ver	*far*
veranderen	*to change*

verantwoordelijk	*responsible*
verbinden	*to connect*
de verbinding	*connection*
verdienen	*to earn*
verdrietig	*sad*
vergelijken	*to compare*
vergeten	*to forget*
(zich) vergissen	*to be mistaken*
de verjaardag	*birthday*
(zich) verkleden	*to change (clothes)*
verkwistend	*wasteful*
verkopen	*to sell*
verkoper	*salesperson*
verlaten	*to leave*
verliefd zijn op	*to be in love with*
(zich) vermaken	*to enjoy oneself*
verpleger (-eegster)	*nurse*
het verschil	*difference*
verschillen	*to differ*
verschillend	*different*
versturen	*to send*
vertrekken	*to depart*
(zich) vervelen	*to get bored*
vervelend	*irritating, a nuisance*
het vervoer	*transport*
de verwarming	*heating*
verwend worden	*to be spoiled*
verzamelen	*to collect*
vieren	*to celebrate*
vies	*dirty*
vinden	*to find*
vindingrijk	*inventive/resourceful*

de vis	*fish*
Vissen	*Pisces*
vlakbij	*close to*
het vlees	*meat*
het vliegveld	*airport*
de vlucht	*flight*
(zich) voelen	*to feel*
de voet	*foot*
het voetbal	*football*
voetballen	*to play football (soccer)*
volgend	*next*
volgens	*according to*
de volle melk	*full fat milk*
voor	*for, before, in front of*
vooraf	*before (time)*
vooral	*especially, above all*
het voorbeeld	*example*
voorbereiden	*to prepare*
het voorgerecht	*hors d'oeuvres, starter*
het voorjaar	*spring*
de voorkeur	*preference*
voorstell en	*to introduce, propose*
vorig	*previous*
de vraag	*question*
vragen	*to ask*
vreemd	*strange*
vreselijk	*terrible/terribly*
de vriend(in)	*friend*
vriendelijk	*friendly*
vriezen	*to freeze*
vrij	*free, fairly*
vroeg	*early*

vrolijk	*jolly*
de vrouw	*woman*
de vuilniszak	*rubbish bag*
waaien	*to blow*
waar	*where*
wachten	*to wait*
de wandeling	*walk*
wanneer	*when*
want	*because*
het warenhuis	*department store*
(zich) wassen	*to wash oneself*
wat	*what*
wat … betreft	*as far as … goes*
Waterman	*Aquarius*
de website-ontwerper	*website designer*
het weer	*weather*
Weegschaal	*Libra*
de week	*week*
de weersverwachting	*weather forecast*
weertje	*(lovely) weather*
de weg	*road*
weggaan	*to go away, leave*
weinig	*few, little*
welk	*which*
het werk	*work*
de werkdruk	*work pressure*
werken	*to work*
weten	*to know*
wie	*who*
de wijn	*wine*
willen	*to want, wish*
de winkel	*shop*

de winkelbediende	shop assistant
winkelen	to shop
wisselen	to (ex)change
wisselend	changeable
het wisselkantoor	bureau de change
wit	white
wonen	to live
worden	to become
de wortel	carrot
zacht	soft, mild
de zak	bag, pocket
het zakdoekje	hanky
zakelijk	regarding business
de zakenman	businessman
de zakenvrouw	businesswoman
het zakje	(small) bag
de zee	sea
de zeep	soap
de zegel	(postage) stamp
zeggen	to say
zeilen	to go sailing
zeker	certain, certainly
zelfs	even
zelfvertrouwen	self-confidence
zetten	to place
zeuren	to nag/complain
ziek	sick
het ziekenhuis	hospital
de ziekte	illness
zien	to see
zijn	to be
zin hebben in/om te	to fancy (doing) something

zitten	*to sit*
zo	*so, like this/that, right away*
zoals	*such as*
zoeken	*to look for*
zoenen	*to kiss*
zoet	*sweet*
de zomer	*summer*
de zon	*sun*
zonder	*without*
zonnig	*sunny*
de zoon	*son*
zorgzaam	*caring*
zout	*salty*
zuid	*south*
zuigen	*to suck*
de zus	*sister*
zuur	*sour*
zwart	*black*
het zwembad	*swimming pool*
zwemmen	*to swim*

English–Dutch vocabulary

(a) little	een beetje
(be) able (vb)	kunnen
about/around	om
above	*boven*
abroad	het buitenland
according	to volgens
account	de rekening
acquaintance	de kennis
active	actief
activity	de activiteit
actor	de acteur
actress	de actrice
address	het adres
administrator	de administrateur
adore (vb)	adoreren
advice (give good advice)	raad (een goede raad geven), het advies
after	na
(in the) afternoon's	middags
against/to	tegen
age	de leeftijd
agreed	afgesproken
air	de lucht
airport	het vliegveld
alarm	clock de wekker
all	allemaal; *all in all* al met al;

all sorts of	allerlei
allow/let (vb)	laten
allowed (be allowed)	mogen
along	langs
already/as early as	al
also	ook
although	(ook) al
always	altijd
ample/considerable	riant
amuse oneself (vb)	(zich) amuseren
analyse (vb)	analyseren
anderen	others
apple	de appel
appointment/arrangement	de afspraak
apricot	de abricoos
Aquarius	Waterman
Aries	Ram
arm	de arm
arrive (vb)	aankomen
art	de kunst
article	het artikel
artist	de kunstenaar (-ares)
artistic	artistiek
as far as … goes	wat … betreft
as much	evenveel
ask (vb)	vragen
aspirin	de aspirine
assistant	de assistent(e), de medewerker (-ster)
at	bij; *at home* thuis; *at night (after midnight)* 's nachts
attractive	aantrekkelijk
aunt	de tante

autumn	de herfst, het najaar
back	de rug
back	terug
bad	slecht
badly	slecht
bag	de tas, zak
bag (small)	het zakje
baker	de bakker
ball	de bal
banana	de banaan
bank	de bank; *bank employee* de bankassistent(e)
bar/pub	de kroeg, de bar, het café
based on	gebaseerd op
basement	het souterrain
be (vb)	zijn
bean	de boon
beautiful	mooi
because	want
become (vb)	worden
become used to (vb)	wennen
beef	het rundvlees
beer	de pils, het bier
before	voor
begin	beginnen
behaviour	het gedrag
belt	de riem
better	beter
between	tussen
bicycle	de fiets
big	groot

birthday	de verjaardag; *it's my birthday* ik ben jarig
biscuit	het koekje
black	zwart
blend / mix (vb)	mengen
blow (vb)	blazen
blow (wind) (vb)	waaien
blue	blauw
body	het lichaam
book (vb)	boeken
book	het boek
booked	geboekt
boot	de laars
bored (to get bored)	(zich) vervelen
boring	saai
born	geboren
borrow	lenen
bossy	bazig
both	allebei
bottle	de fles; *extra charge on glass bottles* het statiegeld
boy	de jongen
boyfriend	de vriend
break	de pauze
breakfast	het ontbijt; *have breakfast (vb)* ontbijten
bring (vb)	brengen; *bring with (vb)* meebrengen
broken	gebroken, kapot
brother	de broer
brown	bruin
bureau de change	het wisselkantoor
bus stop	de bushalte

businessman	de zakenman
businesswoman	de zakenvrouw
busy	druk
but	maar
butcher	de slager
butter	de boter
buy (vb)	kopen
by	bij, door, tegen
cabbage	de kool
cabin	de trekkershut
café	de kroeg, het café, de bar
(be) called (vb)	heten
camp (vb)	kamperen
campsite	de camping
canal (in towns)	de gracht
cancel (an appointment) (vb)	afzeggen
cancel (ticket) (vb)	afstempelen
Cancer	Kreeft
cap	het petje
capital	de hoofdstad
Capricorn	Steenbok
careless/sloppy	onzorgvuldig
caring	zorgzaam
carrot	de wortel
carton	het pak
carry (vb)	dragen
cat	de poes, kat
cauliflower	de bloemkool
celebrate (vb)	vieren
centre (of town)	het centrum
certain	bepaald
certainly	zeker, beslist

chair	de stoel
challenge	de uitdaging
chance	de kans
change	het kleingeld
change (vb)	veranderen; *(buses, etc.)* overstappen; *(clothes)* (zich) verkleden, omkleden; *(money, etc.)* wisselen
changeable	wisselend
characteristic (personal)	de karaktertrek, de karaktereigenschap
chat (vb)	kletsen
cheap	goedkoop
checkout	de kassa
cheese	de jonge kaas
cheese; extra mature	de kaas
cheese; mature	de oude kaas
cheese; young	de belegen kaas
chemist	de drogist
chess (to play chess)	schaken
chicken	de kip
child	het kind (pl. kinderen)
chips (French fries)	de patat, friet
chocolate	de chocola(de)
choice	de keuze
church	de kerk
cinema	de bioscoop
clean (vb)	schoonmaken
clean	schoon
clever	knap, slim
client/customer	de klant
close	to vlakbij
clothes	de kleren (pl.)

cloudy	bewolkt
cod	de kabeljauw
coffee	de koffie
coin	de munt
cold	koel, koud
collect (vb)	afhalen, verzamelen
colour	de kleur
comb	de kam
come (vb)	komen; *come back (vb)* terugkomen; *come with/along (vb)* meekomen
comfortable	comfortabel
comic	de strip
company	het bedrijf; *company culture* de bedrijfscultuur
compare (vb)	vergelijken
compass	het kompas
complicated	ingewikkeld
connect (vb)	verbinden, doorverbinden
connection	de verbinding
conversation	het gesprek
cook (vb)	koken
corner	de hoek
cost (vb)	kosten
cottage/cabin	het huisje
cough	de hoest, hoesten (vb)
country	het land
countryside	het platteland
covered	overdekt
crate	de krat
cream	de room
criticize (vb)	bekritiseren

cross (a road) (vb)	oversteken
crossroads	het kruispunt
curl	de krul
cut (vb)	knippen, snijden
cycle (vb)	fietsen
dance (vb)	dansen
dangerous	gevaarlijk
dark	donker
daughter	de dochter
day	de dag
delicious	lekker, overheerlijk
demanding	veeleisend
dentist	de tandarts
depart (vb)	verstrekken
department	de afdeling
department store	het warenhuis
departure	het vertrek
dessert	het nagerecht, toetje, dessert
differ (vb)	verschillen
difference	het verschil
different	verschillend, anders
difficult	moeilijk
dine (vb)	dineren
direction	de richting
dirty	vies
disciplined	gedisciplineerd
discover (vb)	ontdekken
disguise/camouflage (vb)	camoufleren
dish/meal	de schotel
disturb (vb)	storen
dizziness	duizeligheid
do (vb)	doen

doctor	de dokter
dominate (vb)	domineren
door	de deur
dream (vb)	droom, dromen
dress	de jurk
(get) dressed (vb)	(zich) aankleden
drink	de drank, de borrel
drink (vb)	drinken
drive (vb)	rijden
driver	de chauffeur, bestuurder
dry	droog
dyke	de dijk
each	elk, ieder; each other elkaar
ear	het oor
early	vroeg
earn (vb)	verdienen
easy	makkelijk
eat (vb)	eten
editor	de redacteur
egg	het ei (pl. eieren)
elaborate	uitgebreid
electricity	de electriciteit
embroider	borduren
empty	leeg
end	het eind
endive	de andijvie
energetic	energiek
energy	de energie
enjoy (vb)	genieten
enjoy oneself (vb)	(zich) vermaken
entrance	de ingang
equal	gelijk

especially	vooral
euro	de euro (pl. euro's)
even	zelfs
even though	(ook) al
evening	de avond; in the evening 's avonds
everywhere	overal
example	het voorbeeld;
for example	bijvoorbeeld
excellent	uitstekend
except	behalve
exchange (vb)	wisselen
exciting	boeiend
exercise	de oefening
exhibition	de tentoonstelling
exist (vb)	bestaan
(motorway) exit	de afrit, de afslag
expensive	duur
experience	de ervaring
explain (vb)	verklaren
extensive	uitgebreid
eye	het oog
fairly	tamelijk, redelijk, vrij
fall (vb)	vallen
family	de familie, het gezin; *family life* het familieleven
fanatical	fanatiek
fancy (a boy/girl/doing something) (vb)	gek zijn op; *fancy (doing) something (vb)* zin hebben in/om
fantastic	fantastisch
far	ver
farmer	boer(in)
fashion	de mode

fashionable	modieus
fast	hard, snel
fat	dik
father	de vader
favourite	favoriet
feel (vb)	(zich) voelen
fetch (vb)	halen, ophalen
fever	de koorts
(a) few	een paar
few/little	weinig
filled	gevuld
film	de (speel)film
find (vb)	vinden
finish (vb)	afmaken, eindigen
fish	de vis
flight	de vlucht
flower	de bloem
flu	de griep
food	etenswaren
foot	de voet
football	het voetbal
for	voor
forget (vb)	vergeten
free	vrij
freeze (vb)	vriezen
friend (female)	de vriendin
friend (male)	de vriend
friendly	vriendelijk
from	vanuit, van; from now on voortaan
fry (vb)	bakken
frying pan	de koekepan
fun	leuk; fun to be around gezellig

garden	de tuin
Gemini	Tweelingen
general practitioner	de huisarts
get	krijgen; *get up (vb)* opstaan; *get in/on (vb)* instappen
gherkin	de augurk
gift	het cadeau
girl	het meisje
girlfriend	de vriendin
give (vb)	geven; *give out (vb)* uitreiken
glass	het glas; *glass of beer* het pilsje, biertje
glasses	de bril
go (vb)	gaan; *go away* weggaan; *go out with* gaan met; *go round/ mix with* omgaan
goat's cheese	de geitenkaas
good	goed
good-hearted	goedaardig
good-looking (also clever)	knap
grandma	de oma
grandpa	de opa
grandparent	de grootouder
grape	de druif
green	groen
green bean	de sperzieboon
greengrocer	de groenteboer
grey	grijs
grocer	de kruidenier
guide	de gids
habit	de gewoonte
haddock	de schelvis
hair	het haar

hairdresser's	de kapsalon
hand in (vb)	inleveren
handkerchief	de zakdoek
handle	de knop, het handvat
hang up (vb)	ophangen
hanky	het zakdoekje
haste	de haast
have (vb)	hebben
have to, must (vb)	moeten
hay	fever de hooikoorts
head	het hoofd
headstrong	koppig
healthy	gezond
heating	de verwarming
help (vb)	helpen
here	hier
history	de geschiedenis
holiday	de vakantie
homely	huiselijk
homework	het huiswerk
honest/honourable	integer
horror film	de griezelfilm
hors d'oeuvres	het voorgerecht
hospital	het ziekenhuis
hour	het uur
house	het huis
how	hoe
how much	hoeveel
humour	de humor
hundreds and thousands	de hagelslag
(be) hungry (vb)	honger hebben
hurry (vb)	(zich) haasten

ice, ice cream	het ijs
idea	het idee
ill	ziek
illness	de ziekte
important	belangrijk
in	bij; *in front of* voor
indeed	trouwens
indicate (vb)	aangeven
indecisive	besluiteloos
industrious	ijverig
influence	de invloed
in-line skating	skeeleren
inner peace	de innerlijke rust
inside	binnen
(be) interested (vb)	(zich) interesseren
interesting	interessant
introduce (vb)	voorstellen
inventive/resourceful	vindingrijk
irresistible	onweerstaanbaar
irritate (vb)	irriteren
irritating, a nuisance	vervelend
itch (vb)	jeuken
jacket	de jas, het colbert
jar	de pot
jealous	jaloers
jeans	de spijkerbroek
job	de baan
jolly	vrolijk
journey	de reis
juice	het sap
just	gewoon
key	de sleutel

kiss (vb)	kussen, zoenen
kitchen	de keuken
knit (vb)	breien
know (vb)	weten
knowledge	de kennis
lack of	het gebrek aan
lake	het meer
lamb (meat)	het lamsvlees
language	de taal
late	laat
lawyer	de advocaat
lay/put (vb)	leggen
leader	de leider
learn (vb)	leren
least	minst
leave (vb)	verlaten, weggaan
lecturer	de docent(e)
leek	de prei
left (to the)	links
leg	het been
lend (vb)	lenen
Leo	Leeuw
less	minder
lesson	de les
lettuce	de sla
Libra	Weegschaal
librarian	de bibliothecaris (-esse)
light	het licht, licht (adj.)
light (weight)	licht
like (vb)	ouden van
limit/restrict (vb)	beperken
line	de lijn

liquorice	de drop
list	de lijst
listen (vb)	luisteren
literature	de literatuur
(a) little	een beetje
little, few	weinig
live (vb)	leven; live (in a place, house) wonen
loan	de lening
lobster	de kreeft
local	plaatselijk
lock (canal, etc.)	de sluis
long	lang
look (vb)	kijken; look like eruitzien; look after oppassen; look for/seek zoeken
love	de liefde; to be in love with verliefd zijn op
lovely	heerlijk
loving	liefhebbend
lunch	de lunch; have lunch (vb) lunchen
lunch break	de lunchpauze
machine	de automaat
mad	gek, dol
magazine	het tijdschrift
magnificent	magnifiek
main course	het hoofdgerecht
make (vb)	maken; make an appointment afspreken
man	de man, vent (informal)
manner/way	de manier
many/much	veel
map	de man, kaart
martyr	de martelaar

marvellous	schitterend
matter	de kwestie
meal	de maaltijd
mean (vb)	bedoelen, betekenen
meat	het vlees
medicine	het geneesmiddel, medicijn
meet (vb)	ontmoeten
melon	de meloen
middle	het midden
mild	zacht, mild
milk	de melk; *full fat milk* de volle melk; *semi-skimmed milk* de halfvolle melk;
skimmed milk	de magere melk
mince	het gehakt
minute	de minuut
mistake	de vergissing, fout
(be) mistaken (vb)	(zich) vergissen
mix (with) (vb)	(zich) mengen onder
mobile phone	het mobieltje
moderate	matig
moment	het ogenblik(je)
month	de maand
moody	chagrijnig, humeurig
moors	heidevelden
more	meer
morning	de morgen, ochtend; *in the morning* 's morgens, 's ochtends
most	meest
mother	de moeder
motherly	moederlijk
motorbike	de motor
motorway	de (auto)snelweg

mountain	de berg
mouth	de mond
much/many	veel
municipality	de gemeente
music	de muziek
mussel	de mossel
must, have to (vb)	moeten
nag/complain (vb)	zeuren
name	de naam
nationality	de nationaliteit
natural/naturally	natuurlijk
nature area	het natuurgebied
nature/character	de aard
near	bij
nearly	bijna
neat	net, netjes
necessary	nodig
neck	de hals
necklace	de ketting
neighbourhood	de buurt
network	het netwerk
nevertheless	toch
new	nieuw
newspaper	de krant
next	daarna, volgend; *next one* de volgende; *next to* daarnaast, naast
nice	aardig, prettig
night	de nacht
no	nee, geen
not until	pas
note (money)	het biljet

nothing	niets
now	nu
number	het nummer
nurse	verpleger, verpleegster
obvious	duidelijk
of	van
offer (vb)	(aan)bieden
office	het kantoor
often	vaak
oil	de olie
old	oud
old-fashioned	ouderwets
on	aan
onion	de ui
only	slechts; only one de enige
opinion	de mening
orange (colour)	oranje
orange (fruit)	de sinaasappel
orange juice	de jus d'orange, de sinaasappelsap
order (vb)	bestellen
ordinary, just	gewoon
organize (vb)	organiseren
other	ander
otherwise	anders
out	uit
outside	buiten
overtime	het overwerk
own	eigen
pack/fetch (vb)	pakken
pain	de pijn
paint (vb)	schilderen, verven
paint	de verf

painting	het schilderij
pair	het paar
paper	het papier
parcel	het pakje
parent	de ouder
party	het feest
pass (vb)	passeren
patient	geduldig
pay (vb)	betalen; *pay by card/get money from a cashpoint* pinnen; *pay attention to* letten op
payment	de betaling
pea	de erwt
peach	de perzik
peanut butter	de pindakaas
pear	de peer
perhaps	misschien
permitted	to (vb) mogen
person	de mens, de persoon
personal code	het PINnummer
pharmacist	de apotheek
philosophical	filosofisch
photograph	de foto
pick up (vb)	opnemen
piece	het stuk; *piece of furniture* het meubel
pill	het pilletje, de pil
pin code	de pincode
pineapple	de ananas
Pisces	Vissen
place	de plaats
place (vb)	zetten

plaice	de schol
plain	effen
plastic bag	het plastic tasje
platform	het perron
play (vb)	spelen; play football (soccer) voetballen; play sport sporten; play tennis tennissen
please	graag
pocket	de zak
police	de politie
police station	het politiebureau
policeman	de politieagent
policewoman	de politieagente
polite	beleefd
pork	het varkensvlees
possess (vb)	bezitten
post office	het postkantoor
postcard	de briefkaart
potato	de aardappel
practical	praktisch
(doctor's) practice	de praktijk
prawn	de garnaal
preference	de voorkeur
prepare (vb)	voorbereiden
prepared	bereid
prescription	het recept
present	cadeau(tje), kado(otje) (old spelling) press/print (vb) drukken
pretentious	pretentieus
pretty	fraai
previous	vorig
priority	de prioriteit

private	privé
problem	het probleem
profession	het beroep
programme	het programma
project	het project
propose (vb)	voorstellen
public	openbaar
punctual	punctueel
purple	paars
put/lay (vb)	leggen
quarter	het kwart
question	de vraag
quiet	rustig, stil
quite	nogal, vrij tanelijk
radish	de radijs
railway	de spoorweg; railway timetable het spoorboekje
rain	de regen
raspberry	de framboos
rather	liever
react to (vb)	reageren op
read (vb)	lezen
(be) ready (vb)	klaar staan
real/really	echt
really/actually	eigenlijk
reason	de reden
reasonable	redelijk
recipe	het recept
red	rood
relationship	de relatie
relax (vb)	ontspannen
reliable	betrouwbaar

repair (vb)	repareren
repeat (vb)	herhalen
responsible	verantwoordelijk
result	de uitslag, het gevolg
return	het retour
rice	de rijst
right (to the)	rechts
ring (vb)	bellen; *ring up* opbellen
risk	het risico
road	de weg
(bread) roll	het bolletje, het broodje; *(crusty) roll* het puntje
romantic	romantisch
room	de kamer
round	rond
round off (vb)	afronden
roundabout	de rotonde
route/line	de lijn
rubbish	het afval; *rubbish bag* de vuilniszak
rucksack	de rugzak
Sagittarius	Boogschutter
sail (vb)	zeilen; *sailing boat* varen
sailing boat	zeilboot
salesperson (male)	verkoper, *(female)* verkoopster
salty	zout
sandwich	de boterham
save (vb)	sparen
say (vb)	zeggen
Scorpio	Schorpioen
scream (vb)	schreeuwen
sea	de zee
season	het jaargetijde

secondhand	tweedehands
secretary	de secretaresse
see (vb)	zien
seem (vb)	schijnen
self-confidence	zelfvertrouwen
selfish	egoïstisch
sell (vb)	verkopen
send (vb)	versturen; send an
email	emailen
sense/feeling	het gevoel
sensitive	gevoelig
service	de dienst
share (vb)	delen
shirt	het overhemd
shoe	de schoen
shop (vb)	winkelen
shop	de winkel
shop assistant	de winkelbediende
shopping	de boodschappen
short	kort
shower (of rain)	de bui
shut	dicht
sick	misselijk
sick/ill	ziek
since	sinds
single	enkel
sister	de zus
sit (vb)	zitten
size	de maat
skate (vb)	schaatsen
skirt	de rok
sleep	slapen

sleeping bag	de slaapzak
sleeve	de mouw
slice	het plakje
slim	slank
slow	traag
slowly	langzaam
small	klein
small-minded	kleinzielig
smart/clever	slim
smile (vb)	glimlachen
snack	het hapje
snow (vb)	sneeuwen
snow	de sneeuw
so/thus	dus
soap	de zeep
sociable	sociaal
soft	zacht
solve (vb)	oplossen
someone	iemand
something	iets
sometimes	soms
somewhere	ergens
son	de zoon
soon	straks
soup	de soep
sour	zuur
south	zuid
sparkling mineral water	spa rood
speak (vb)	spreken, praten
spend (vb)	uitgeven
spinach	de spinazie
spiritual	spiritueel

(be) spoiled (vb)	verwend worden
spread (vb)	smeren
spring	de lente, het voorjaar
spring roll	de loempia
stage	het toneel
stairs	de trap
stamp (a ticket) (vb)	afstempelen
(postage) stamp	de (post)zegel
stand (vb)	staan
starter	het voorgerecht
station	het station; *station buffet* de restauratie
stay (vb)	blijven; *stay (with someone)* logeren
steak	de biefstuk
stick/jam (vb)	klemmen
stiff	stijf
still/yet	nog
still mineral water	spa blauw
stomach	de buik, de maag
stop (vb)	stoppen
store	de winkel
storm (vb)	onweer, stormen
straight on	rechtdoor
straightaway	meteen, direct
strange	raar, vreemd
strawberry	de aardbei
street	de straat
strength	de kracht
striped	gestreept
strong	sterk
student	de studente; *fellow student* de medestudente

studies	de studie
study (vb)	studeren
stupid	dom
such as	zoals
suck (vb)	zuigen
sugar	de suiker
suit	het pak
suitcase	de koffer
summer	de zomer
sun	de zon
sunny	zonnig
supermarket	de supermarkt
surgery	het spreekuur
surroundings	de omgeving
sweater	de trui
sweet	het snoepje
sweet/nice	zoet
swim (vb)	zwemmen
swimming pool	het zwembad
sympathetic	sympathiek
symptom	het symptoom
system	het systeem
table	de tafel
tactful	tactvol
take (vb)	nemen; take with meenemen
talk (vb)	praten, spreken
taste (vb)	smaken
tasty	lekker
Taurus	Stier
tea	de thee
teach (vb)	leren
teacher	de leraar (-ares)

team (of 11)	het elftal
telephone	de telefoon
telephone number	het telefoonnummer
tendency	de neiging
terrible/terribly	vreselijk
terrific	geweldig
text	de tekst
thank (vb)	danken
thanks	bedankt
that	dat
theatre	het theater, de schouwburg
theme park	het pretpark
then	dan
there	daar, er
thin	dun, mager
thing	het ding
things, a great many	heel veel
think (vb)	denken; *think about* nadenken
(be) thirsty (vb)	dorst hebben
this	dit; *this afternoon* vanmiddag; *this evening* vanavond; *this morning* vanmorgen, vanochtend
this, these	deze
though	ook al
throat	de keel
throw (vb)	gooien
thunderstorm	deonweersbui
ticket	het kaartje, de kaart; *ticket clerk* de lokettist(e); *ticket office* het loket
tidy/neat	netjes
tie (neck-)	de stropdas

tight	strak
time	de tijd
times	keer
tired	moe
to	naar, aan
to (up to, as far as)	tot
today	vandaag
together	samen
tomato	de tomaat
tomorrow	morgen
toothbrush	de tandenborstel
toothpaste	de tandpasta
town	de stad (pl. steden)
traffic jam	de file
train	de trein
transport	het vervoer
travel (vb)	reizen; *travel agent* het reisbureau
trip	de tocht, het uitstapje
trousers	de broek
try on (vb)	passen
tub	het kuipje
turn (my turn)	de beurt (mijn beurt)
turn/time	de keer
type	het soort
uncle	de oom
uncompromising	star
understand (vb)	begrijpen
undress (vb)	uitkleden
unfortunate	helaas
ungrateful	ondankbaar
university de	universiteit
urgent	dringend

use (vb)	gebruiken
(get) used to (vb)	wennen
usually	meestal
valid	geldig
vegetables	de groente
very	heel
view	het uitzicht
village	het dorp
Virgo	Maagd
visit	het bezoek
visit (vb)	opzoeken
vulnerability	kwetsbaarheid
vulnerable	kwetsbaar
wait (vb)	wachten
waiter	de ober
walk	de wandeling
walk (vb)	lopen, wandelen; walk (a dog) uitlaten
want/wish (vb)	willen
warm/affectionate	hartelijk
wash oneself (vb)	(zich) wassen
wasteful	verkwistend
way/manner	de manier
wear (vb)	dragen
weather	het weer; (lovely) weather weertje
weather forecast	de weersverwachting
website designer	de websiteontwerper
week	de week
weight	het gewicht
wet	nat
what	wat
when	wanneer

where	waar
which	welk(e)
white	wit
who	wie
whole	heel
window	het raam
wine	de wijn
without	zonder
woman	de vrouw
wonderful	prachtig, schitterend
woods	bossen
work	het werk; *work pressure* de werkdruk
work (vb)	werken
write (vb)	schrijven; *write down* opschrijven
year	het jaar
yellow	geel
yet/still	nog
young	jong

"Global scale" of the Common European Framework of Reference for Languages: learning, teaching, assessment (CEFR)

Advanced	**CEFR LEVEL C2**	Can understand with ease virtually everything heard or read. Can summarise information from different spoken and written sources, reconstructing arguments and accounts in a coherent presentation. Can express him/herself spontaneously, very fluently and precisely, differentiating finer shades of meaning even in more complex situations.
Advanced	**CEFR LEVEL C1**	Can understand a wide range of demanding, longer texts, and recognise implicit meaning. Can express him/herself fluently and spontaneously without much obvious searching for expressions. Can use language flexibly and effectively for social, academic and professional purposes. Can produce clear, well-structured, detailed text on complex subjects, showing controlled use of organisational patterns, connectors and cohesive devices.
Intermediate	**CEFR LEVEL B2 (A Level)**	Can understand the main ideas of complex text on both concrete and abstract topics, including technical discussions in his/her field of specialisation. Can interact with a degree of fluency and spontaneity that makes regular interaction with native speakers quite possible without strain for either party. Can produce clear, detailed text on a wide range of subjects and explain a viewpoint on a topical issue giving the advantages and disadvantages of various options.
Intermediate	**CEFR LEVEL B1 (Higher GCSE)**	Can understand the main points of clear standard input on familiar matters regularly encountered in work, school, leisure, etc. Can deal with most situations likely to arise whilst travelling in an area where the language is spoken. Can produce simple connected text on topics which are familiar or of personal interest. Can describe experiences and events, dreams, hopes and ambitions and briefly give reasons and explanations for opinions and plans.
Beginner	**CEFR LEVEL A2: (Foundation GCSE)**	Can understand sentences and frequently used expressions related to areas of most immediate relevance (e.g. very basic personal and family information, shopping, local geography, employment). Can communicate in simple and routine tasks requiring a simple and direct exchange of information on familiar and routine matters. Can describe in simple terms aspects of his/her background, immediate environment and matters in areas of immediate need.
Beginner	**CEFR LEVEL A1**	Can understand and use familiar everyday expressions and very basic phrases aimed at the satisfaction of needs of a concrete type. Can introduce him/herself and others and can ask and answer questions about personal details such as where he/she lives, people he/she knows and things he/she has. Can interact in a simple way provided the other person talks slowly and clearly and is prepared to help.

For learning on the go download our *Get Started in Dutch* companion app:

Dutch: Teach Yourself

- **Choose how you learn** – our apps follow the same unit structure as our courses, so you can get extra practice wherever and whenever you want.

- **Make learning fun** – our apps are packed with interactive activities that give you immediate feedback.

- **Take your learning further** – compare your spoken answers and pronunciation to recordings of native speakers with our unique record and compare feature.

- **Listen as you learn** – our apps include full audio to accompany dialogues and listening exercises.

- **Control your learning** – track your progress and your scores to quickly identify what you need to review.

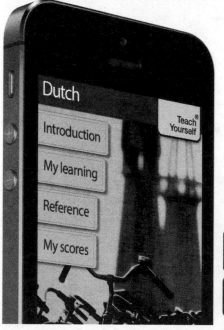

Picture credits

Picture credits